GERMAN

Edith Baer and
Margaret Wightman

...has printed ...ished continuously since 1584.

Cambridge University Press

Cambridge

London   New York   New Rochelle

Melbourne   Sydney

Published by the Press Syndicate of the University of Cambridge
The Pitt Building, Trumpington Street, Cambridge CB2 1RP
32 East 57th Street, New York, NY 10022, U S A
10 Stamford Road, Oakleigh, Melbourne 3166, Australia

First published 1982
Sixth printing 1987

Printed in Hong Kong by
Wing King Tong

ISBN 0 521 28186 5

Acknowledgements

The majority of the photographs in this book were taken in
West Germany by the authors.

Thanks are due to the following for permission to reproduce
copyright material:

p 21 *auf 1200m Vorsicht beim Überholen* Deutsche
Verkehrswacht, Bonn; p 23 *Grüne Welle* 'IVB Report' Düsseldorf;
p 25 *Rheinbrücke*, p 83 *Gaststätte zum schwarzen Bären* Presse-
und Informationsamt der Bundesregierung, Bundesbildstelle, Bonn;
p 39 *H* Stadtwerke·München Verkehrsbetriebe, foto: Lorenz;
p 40 *Fahrpreis wählen!*, p 42 *Einzelfahrkarten/Mehrfahrtenkarten*
Süddeutscher Verlag, Munich; p. 52 post office symbol Bild-Archiv
des Bundes-Ministerium für Post- und Fernmeldewesen, Bonn.

What this book is about

* It helps you — even if you're a beginner — to understand the signs and notices that will confront you on a visit to Germany.
* It shows you how to get the gist of them without having to worry about the meaning of every single word.
* It contains plenty of practice material so that you can check your progress.
* It gives you an idea of how the German language works.
* It provides some unusual and unexpected insights into German attitudes.

How the book works

'Finding your way through the forest of signs' gives you some general ideas on how to make sense of signs and on how to judge whether they're important to you or not. This part includes notes about the way the language on signs works and tells you which words to look out for and how to sort out the different types of sign.

Chapters 1—14 deal with situations you may have to cope with and the signs you're likely to come across. Each chapter has a 'Key words' section, listing those words you'll find most useful, explanations of important signs and some 'Test yourself' questions for self-checking. For easy reference and revision there's a word list on p 100.

How to use it

* First go carefully through 'The forest of signs'. You can then take the individual chapters in any order; they are self-contained. You may find it a help to re-read 'The forest of signs' before tackling a new chapter.
* Once you've studied the 'Key words' of the chapter, try to memorise them. Then go on to the section introducing the signs. Concentrate on getting the gist as you would need to in a real-life situation. Resist the temptation of puzzling out every word.
* Finally try the 'Test yourself' questions at the end of the chapter and check your answers with the Key on p 97.

CONTENTS

4

FINDING YOUR WAY THROUGH THE FOREST OF SIGNS

In Germany almost every area of public life is thoroughly signposted. There are signs to warn you, to ask you to do – or not to do – something, to help you on your way, or sometimes to state the obvious. Signs often flash by and you need to 'get the message' quickly. Many are written in a style of language – a form of officialese – that you will not meet in everyday speech or want to use yourself, and a dictionary won't always help. So to get to grips with signs and notices you need to develop a special technique.

1 Ignore very long signs

They often contain detailed instructions or regulations in legal jargon. Attach more importance to bold lettering than small print. On this sign the only word that matters is **Privatparkplatz** (private car park).

PRIVATPARKPLATZ!
Es gelten die Vorschriften der Straßenverkehrsordnung
Höchstgeschwindigkeit 15 km/h
Unberechtigt parkende Fahrzeuge werden kostenpflichtig abgeschleppt
Gemeinschaftswerk Hattingen GmbH

Concentrate on the shorter signs
>**zu den Bussen** (to the buses)
>**heute Ruhetag** (closing day today)

2 Sort out the different types of sign

Signs with **Achtung** (beware), **Vorsicht** (careful) or ! urge you *to take care*:
>**Unfall!** (accident)
>**Vorsicht Tram** (careful – tram)
>**Achtung Diebstahlgefahr** (beware of thieves)

One-word signs often *direct* you **to a place**:
>**Bahnhof** (station)
>**Stadtmitte** (town centre)

Signs with **bitte** (please) are *requests*:
>**bitte läuten** (please ring)
>**bitte Motor abstellen** (please switch off the engine)

Signs with **nicht** (not) or **bitte nicht** ask you *not to do* something:
>**nicht rauchen** (no smoking)
>**bitte nicht läuten** (please don't ring)

Signs with **kein** or **keine** (no) tell you something *can't* or *shouldn't be done*:

 kein Ausgang (no exit)
 keine Einfahrt (no entry for vehicles)

Signs with **verboten** or **Verbot** *forbid* you to do something (see also p 10):

 Parkverbot (parking prohibited)
 Rauchen verboten (smoking prohibited)

? TEST YOURSELF (Answers on p 97)

Which sign (i) asks you not to do something (ii) asks you to do something (iii) tells you to take care (iv) shows you the way (v) informs you that something shouldn't be used (vi) forbids you to do something?

a

KEIN √ EINGANG

b
·BITTE NICHT RAUCHEN· /

c
Achtung! /// Schranke!

d

Parken √/ verboten

e

⚠ Messe /v

f

Bitte diese Tür immer schließen //

3 Pick out the 'key words'

The word that can give you a clue to the meaning of a sign is often made up of two or more words. One part of it may provide the key, e.g. **Badeplatz: baden** (to bathe) + **Platz** (place) = bathing area. So **Bade. . .** tells you the sign has to do with bathing.

Once you can spot a 'key word', you can often work out what a sign is about. When you're motoring or travelling around, words with **Fahr. . .** and **. . .fahrt** (**fahren**, to travel) could be 'key words':

 Abfahrt (departure)
 Busfahrt (bus trip)
 Fahrbahn (roadway)
 Fahrkarte (travel ticket)

NÄCHSTE ABFAHRT 13³⁵

nächste next *ExiT*

If you're sightseeing then words with **Tag** (day) may be important; they can indicate a day of the week (see p 10), time of day, or something valid for a day:

 feiertags (on public holidays)
 Mittag (midday)
 Sonntag (Sunday)
 Tageskarte (day ticket)

You'll find a list of key words at the beginning of each chapter.

THEATERKASSE
SONN- U. FEIERTAGS
VON 11-13 UHR
GEÖFFNET

Theaterkasse theatre box office
sonn- = **sonntags** on Sundays

7

4 Look for other words that matter

They can also give you a clue as to what the sign is about and help you to decide whether it concerns you or not. They appear on many signs, so try to memorise these words and expressions:

* **auf eigene Gefahr** means you're doing something at your own risk (if anything happens to you the legal liability is yours):
Durchgang auf eigene Gefahr (way through at your risk)

* **betreten** (to step on to) is usually coupled with **nicht** or **verboten**, and warns you to keep out of a place:
Betreten der Baustelle verboten (do not enter construction site)

* **frei** tells you that something is free, available or exempt:
gebührenfrei (free of charge)
Zimmer frei (rooms available)
Anlieger frei (residents exempt)

* **geöffnet** means a place is open
* **geschlossen** tells you it's closed

* **Hund** or **Hunde** (dog/s): you can ignore the sign — unless you have a dog with you or the sign is on someone's front gate (then it's a warning):
Hunde an die Leine (put dogs on a lead)
Warnung vor dem Hunde (beware of the dog)

* **Kinder** (children): another sign you can ignore, unless you travel with children or drive a car:
Kinderspielplatz (children's playground)
Vorsicht Schulkinder (careful — school children)

* **nur** means 'only'; it helps you to spot whether you're among the 'privileged':
nur für Hotelgäste (for hotel guests only)
or draws your attention to a bargain:
Rosen Stück nur 1.- DM (roses only 1 mark each)

* **zu den, zum, zur** (to the) appear on signs that direct you to a place:
    zu den Toiletten (to the toilets)
    zum Zoo (to the zoo)
    zur Kirche (to the church)

? TEST YOURSELF

Which of these signs would concern you if you (i) spotted a swimming pool in a hotel and wanted to swim there (ii) had a dog with you (iii) wanted to know when the car park is open (iv) would like to take your small daughter to the playground (v) were looking for the counter where they sell day tickets (vi) wanted to get a train ticket?

a

b

c  d e

f

5 Look at the way the 'sign' language works

It's likely to be an *instruction* if the last word ends in . . .**en**; that's the word telling you what to do or not to do:
    Knopf <u>drücken</u> (press)
    Einfahrt <u>freihalten</u> (keep clear)
    Teppich <u>nicht</u> <u>betreten</u> (don't walk on)
Then look what you're to use, press etc.:
    <u>Knopf</u> drücken (button)
    <u>Einfahrt</u> freihalten (entrance)
    <u>Teppich</u> nicht betreten (carpet)
If **zu** (to) appears before the last word or in the middle of it, it's extra emphatic:
    Kinder sind an der Hand <u>zu führen</u> (children must be taken by the hand)
    Einfahrt ist <u>freizuhalten</u> (entrance must be kept clear)

It's certain to be a *prohibition* if the sign ends in **verboten, untersagt** (prohibited), **nicht gestattet, nicht erlaubt** (not allowed). *What* you're not permitted to do usually comes first:

Feuer und Rauchen polizeilich verboten (naked lights and smoking prohibited by the police) (This sign is displayed in many garages.)

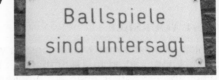

Ballspiele sind untersagt (ball games are forbidden)

Radfahren im Park nicht gestattet (cycling not allowed in the park)

You'll notice that a great many things are forbidden in Germany! As a rule such things are spelt out very clearly and are not left to people's common sense.

? TEST YOURSELF

Which signs are instructions and which are prohibitions? (Don't attempt to make sense of every word.)

a

b

c

d

e

f
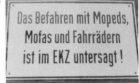

6 Other things you need to recognise

Days of the week

They also appear in shortened forms:

Monday	**Montag** or **Mo**	Friday	**Freitag, Frei** or **Fr**
Tuesday	**Dienstag, Die** or **Di**	Saturday	**Samstag, Samst** or **Sa**
Wednesday	**Mittwoch** or **Mi**		**Sonnabend** (in North Germany)
Thursday	**Donnerstag** or **Do**	Sunday	**Sonntag** or **So**

Look out also for **Feiertag** (public holiday), **werktags** (on weekdays) and **täglich, tägl.** or **tgl.** (daily).

Other short forms

These are included in the word list at the back. Two that you'll see frequently are **Str.** = **Strasse** (street) and **u.** = **und** (and). You'll also need to recognise

10

the brief way of writing pairs of similar words:

    Ein- und Ausfahrt = Einfahrt und Ausfahrt
    In- und Ausland = Inland und Ausland
    sonn- u. feiertags = sonntags und feiertags

Numbers

1st, 2nd, 3rd etc. appear as 1., 2., 3. or sometimes I., II., III. etc. An **m** after a number means 'metres' (not miles!) e.g. **50m** = 50 metres.

Times

The 24-hour system is in use everywhere:

    13.00 or **13.00 Uhr** = 1 pm
    19.30 or **19.30 Uhr** = 7.30 pm
    00.00 or **24.00 Uhr** = midnight

Sometimes you see **h** instead of **Uhr** (o'clock) e.g. **7.00h**.
Stunde or **Std.** is an hour, **2 Std.** is two hours.

Money

Prices can be written in several ways:

    DM 20. DM 20.- 20.- 20.00 20DM = 20 marks
    DM .20 .20DM 0.20 -,20 20 20Pf = 20 pfennigs.

This sign ₰ also means pfennig.

Be careful — a comma is often used instead of a decimal point.

Tafel bar

Lettering and writing

Old-fashioned Gothic lettering is now used mainly on ornamental signs as on this one advertising a wine harvesting festival (**Weinlesefest**). Notice the letter 's' and the capital 'W'.

Other examples are given on pp 55, 64, 83, 86, 87.

The symbol ß (= **ss**) is still widely used. It appears as **ss** in the text of this book. You'll also need to recognise the handwritten sign ℔ for the pound or ½ kilogram.

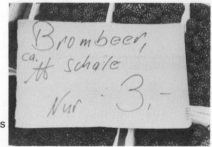

Brombeer blackberries
Schale   carton

Note that the figures 1 and 7 are often written 1 and 7.
Many signs are entirely in capital letters, but in the text we have put capital letters only where they would normally be used.

7 Recognise different forms of the same word

Key words and other essential vocabulary are listed in the word list in their basic form. You'll notice many variations. An extra **-e**, **-en**, **-er**, **-n** or two dots over a vowel often indicate a plural:

Gleis (platform)
zu den Gleisen (to the platforms)
Zug (train)
zu den Zügen (to the trains)

The endings of adjectives also vary:

neues und altes Schloss (old and new castle)
zum neuen und alten Schloss (to the old and new castle)

You'll come across various forms of the word for 'the': **der**, **die**, **das**, **den**; **dem** is 'to the'; **des** is 'of the'.

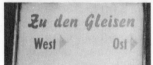

8 Get to know these three-letter words . . .

auf on, for
bis until, up to
für or **f.** for
mit or **m.** with
von or **v.** from
vor in front of, before

. . . and two letter words

ab from, departing from
am at the, by the
an or **a.** at
im in the
in or **i.** in
zu to

1 GETTING AROUND ON FOOT

🅠 KEY WORDS

Fuss (foot)	shows you which routes and areas are reserved for pedestrians (**Fussgänger**): **Fussgängerstrasse, Fussgängerzone** (pedestrian precinct) **Fussgängerweg, Fussweg** (footpath)
. . . gang (way, passage)	points the way in, out etc. if you're on foot: **Ausgang** (way out) — **Notausgang** (emergency exit) **Durchgang** (way through) **Eingang** (way in) **Übergang** (way across) **Zugang** (way to, access)
Geh . . . (**gehen**, to walk)	tells you where to walk: **Gehbahn, Gehweg** (pavement)
. . . tritt (step)	means you're stepping into a place: **Eintritt** (entrance) **Zutritt** (access) You'll often see them with **nur, kein** or **verboten** in which case you probably won't be able to go in: **kein Eintritt** (no entry), **Zutritt verboten** (access prohibited), **Eintritt nur für Mitglieder** (members only)
Weg (way, path)	indicates a way for pedestrians: **Fussweg** (footpath) **Gehweg** (pavement) **öffentlicher Weg** (public footpath) **Rundweg** (path that takes you back to your starting point) *but* **. . .weg** at the end of a street name doesn't mean there's no traffic!

OTHER IMPORTANT WORDS

links (left, on the left)   **rechts** (right, on the right)
um die Ecke (round the corner)

Going the right way

Look for:

* one-word signs, usually black on white, sometimes white on green

Stadtmitte town centre

* words ending in . . .**gang**

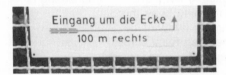

Brücke bridge

* **Weg** or words ending in . . .**weg**

Schwimmbad swimming pool

* signs starting with **zu den**, **zum** or **zur** (to the)

Stadtmauer town wall

Other words that help you find your way around are street names (signs are white on deep blue or black on white); common endings are . . .**strasse**, . . .**str.** (street), . . .**gasse** (lane), . . .**allee** (avenue), . . .**weg** (way), . . .**platz**, . . .**pl.** (square).

(See also p 23.)

Crossing the road

Traffic lights for pedestrians must be observed. It's an offence to cross against the 'red'. Press the button when you see this sign.

drücken push
Grün abwarten
wait for green

You may be told to wait until the road is completely clear.

warten wait
Fahrbahn roadway

Sometimes you're not allowed to cross at all. Instead you have to use (**benützen** or **benutzen**) a subway (**Unterführung**).

hier here

Occasionally you're told to use the pavement on the other side of the road.

gegenüber opposite

As you walk along the pavement you'll notice that most people keep to the right. You'll also notice that as a rule a man walks on the left of a woman.

Finding your way into a building

Look for **Eingang** or **Eintritt**.

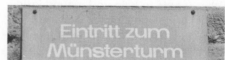

Münsterturm cathedral tower

Where you see **drücken** on a door you push, when it says **ziehen** you pull; **läuten** or **klingeln** means that you should ring.

This isn't the name of the firm or the house owner — it means 'bell'!

In offices, factories, official buildings, visitors (**Besucher**) may have to report (**anmelden**) to the doorkeeper or to reception.

. . . around a building

Inside a building you may need to find the stairs (**Treppe**), the lift (**Aufzug**, **Lift** or **Fahrstuhl**) or the escalator (**Rolltreppe** or **Fahrtreppe**).

In large buildings and in lifts the various floors are described as **Erdgeschoss** (ground floor), **Obergeschoss** (upper floor) and **Untergeschoss** or **Tiefgeschoss** (basement). But on signs outside buildings the floors are generally called **Stock** or — particularly in Southern Germany — **Etage**.

Wegweiser sign board

Bechtel name of firm

Other words to help you around inside buildings include **Zimmer** or **Räume** (rooms), **Büro** (office), . . .**amt** (department).

nebenan next door

. . . and out again

Make for **Ausgang!**

Watch how you go

Take care where it says **Vorsicht** or **Achtung**.

Stufe step

Fahrzeugverkehr traffic

Avoid going where you see:

* **kein** (no) with a key word, e.g. **kein Durchgang** (no way through)
* **nicht betreten** (keep off or out)

Rasen lawn

* **Unbefugte** (unauthorised persons) and of course **verboten**

* or a warning about a dog. The most common signs are **Warnung vor dem Hunde** or this sign.

bissiger fierce

Remember the risk is yours when it says **auf eigene Gefahr.**

Benutzung use

(For **Gefahr** meaning 'danger' see chapter 14 p 93.)

❓ TEST YOURSELF

Before you attempt the questions go over the chapter again and 'Finding your way through the forest of signs'.

1 If you're visiting a business friend at work which sign do you look for first?

a

b

2 What are you not allowed to do here? *Walk Through*

3 **Tür** means door. What should or shouldn't you do to enter?

BITTE NICHT LAUTEN
TÜR DRÜCKEN

4 What do these signs tell you?

a

EINGANG UM DIE ECKE

Entrance around the corner

b

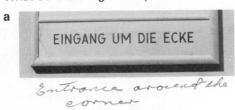

*Here no overpass.
arrow shows
where.*

5 These signs are at the entrance of office blocks. How much notice would you take of them if you wanted to go in?

a

'Kein Zutritt für Hunde'

b

Besucher müssen sich anmelden

no dogs allowed.

6 Which direction should you take?

a

 *Right*

b

 *Left*

7 Mainau island (**Insel**) is no ordinary island. How will you get there?

footpath

8 What do these signs tell you about the escalator?

a

b

9 What's the difference between these signs near a footbridge (**Steg**)?

a

b

Innocent abroad

IF THAT'S THE **EXIT** I'M NOT TAKING THE PLUNGE!

2 MOTORING

a Going the right way (See also chapter 1.)

KEY WORDS

fahren
(to travel)

Fahr. . . has to do with the roadway itself, and the people or vehicles using it:
Fahrbahn (roadway)
Fahrer (driver) — **Autofahrer** (motorist), **Radfahrer** (cyclist)
Fahrrad (bicycle)
Fahrzeug (vehicle)

. . .**fahrt** points the way in, out etc. for a vehicle:
Ausfahrt (exit)
Durchfahrt (way through)
Einfahrt (entry)
Zufahrt (access)
but **Vorfahrt** means priority or right of way

Verkehr
(traffic)

what comes before it tells you what kind of traffic:
Anliegerverkehr (residents' vehicles)
Begegnungsverkehr, **Gegenverkehr** (oncoming traffic)
Durchgangsverkehr (through traffic)
Lieferverkehr (tradesmen's vehicles)
Linksverkehr (traffic on the left)

OTHER IMPORTANT WORDS

Fussgänger (pedestrians)　**Strassenbahn** (tram)

Hiring a car

If you want to hire a car, look for
Autovermietung (**vermieten** = to hire out).

The colour of direction signs

Yellow background: for main roads. The number on its own is the road number, the number + **km** means the distance in kilometres.

White background: for districts and places within towns.

Stadtteil district　　**Flughafen** airport

Blue background: for motorways and roads leading to them.

The rule of the road

Priority

Road sign symbols are mostly the same as in Britain. But this one (yellow on white) is an important exception: it means you're on a priority road (**Vorfahrtstrasse**). A black line through it marks the end of the priority road.

Traffic from the right has priority at junctions when there is no priority sign. There are occasional reminders: **Vorfahrt achten** (pay attention to priority), **Vorfahrt gewähren** (give way), or warnings of a recent change in priority.

geändert changed

Vorrang means right of way for certain road users. The word at the beginning of the sign tells you which ones.

hat has

Pedestrian precinct signs usually say **Fussgänger haben Vorrang** (pedestrians have right of way).

Overtaking

You drive on the right (**rechts fahren**) and overtake (**überholen**) all vehicles on the left (**links**), except trams.

beim when

Some 'no overtaking' signs allow exceptions. Look for **frei** (exempt), **ausgenommen** (except) or **dürfen überholt werden** (may be overtaken). You may often overtake tractors (**Zugmaschinen**). Note: **Zugmaschinen** has nothing to do with **Zug** meaning train!

21

Direction signs you must observe

One-way street (white arrow on blue).

Diversion (black on yellow).

'No entry' except for. . .

Many 'all vehicles prohibited' signs carry words exempting some road users. Look for **frei**, **frei für** or **ausgenommen**. For example, **Anlieger** (residents) or **Anliegerverkehr** could include you if you're visiting a resident.

Another exception that could affect you is **Besucher** (visitors).

If you're going to a specific place see if the sign says **frei bis** (exempt as far as) and the name of the place.

Driving in towns

The (black on yellow) sign at the beginning of a town or village gives you its name and acts as a speed limit sign (i.e. 50 kilometres per hour, or 30 mph, in a built-up area).

Landkreis district
(Other words are place names)

At the end of the town a sign with a diagonal red line through it ends the speed restriction.

To get to the town centre follow
Stadtmitte, Innenstadt or **Zentrum**
but **Einkaufszentrum** is a shopping
centre, **Badezentrum** a swimming centre.
Some towns have expressways right
into the centre; look for **Autostrasse** or
Schnellweg. Or there may be an
alternative fast route into town.

so geht's schneller it's quicker
this way

To take the best route right through the
town follow the signs **Fernverkehr** or
Durchgangsverkehr (long-distance
traffic).
In big cities you may see a sign **Grüne
Welle** (green wave) with a
recommended speed: at this speed you'll
meet all traffic lights on that road at
green.

bei at

Looking for a particular building or place

. . .**haus** (house) or . . .**halle** (hall) may
be clues:

    Kongresshaus congress centre
    Krankenhaus hospital
    Rathaus town hall
    Ausstellungshalle exhibition hall
    Messehalle trade fair centre
    Stadthalle civic hall

Other places you may want to find are the airport (**Flughafen**), the car ferry
(**Autofähre**), a particular bridge (**Brücke**), a car park (**Parkplatz**), a camp site
(**Campingplatz**).

You may also want a specialised area
(**Gebiet**), e.g. **Industriegebiet** (industrial
estate), **Gewerbegebiet** (trading estate).

When you're getting close to the place
you want, there may be signs for access
or entrance. Look for words with
. . .**fahrt**.

Häusern houses

Areas and roads that are closed or restricted

Schranke warns you of a barrier ahead.

Sperrzone or gesperrt tells you the road or area is closed to traffic. So does a sign with Fussgängerzone. (See also chapter 1, p 13.)

In other Zonen you need to take special care, e.g. in a Lärmschutzzone (noise control area) where no noise is permitted at night.

Things you're requested to do

* bitte Motor abstellen (please switch off engine). Note: Motor is never a motor car!
* Schritt fahren (dead slow) (Schritt = pace)
* leiser fahren (drive more quietly)
* einordnen (get in lane)

* bitte Abstand halten (please keep your distance)

  You often see this on the back of a tram – you ignore it at your peril!

  grosser Kurvenausschlag swings wide on bends

A sign that may puzzle you

It means that schoolboys or girls, specially trained as crossing patrols (**Schülerlotsen**) may stop the traffic to let schoolchildren pass.

❓ TEST YOURSELF

1 Where do you get to if you follow these signs?

a

b

Flughafen

c

2 You're driving down a narrow road through a wood. Which type of vehicle are you allowed to overtake?

3 This sign near the ferry boat asks you to move up close (**dicht aufrücken**). What else?

> Bitte dicht aufrücken
> Motor abstellen

4 What does this sign at the entrance to a camp site tell you?

> Campingbesucher keine Durchfahrt
> Parken nur am Parkplatz

5 If you want to park here what
  should you do?

6 Why are you told to take care?

a
b
c

7 You want to spend the afternoon by
  the lake (**See**). Which words tell you
  that you can get there by car?

8 You may not understand every word
  of this sign in the rear window of a
  car, but it has a message for you.
  What is it?

9 Which vehicles are allowed to use
  this part of the road?

10 How far can you go past this 'no
   entry' sign?

b Finding somewhere to park

KEY WORDS

Gebühr (charge)	**gebührenfrei** (free of charge) **gebührenpflichtig** (charge payable) **Parkgebühr** (parking fee)
parken (to park)	**Parkhaus** (multi-storey car park) **Parkplatz** (car park – also parking space) **Parkschein** (ticket for parking)

SYMBOLS WORTH KNOWING

 parking under cover
(white on blue)

 parking disc required
(white on blue)

Most other symbols for parking and no-parking are the same as in Britain.

Names of different types of vehicle

Useful if you want to know whether a parking restriction applies to you or not.

Four-wheelers

Wagen (car)

Lkw (= **Lastkraftwagen**) official jargon for lorry
Pkw (= **Personenkraftwagen**) official jargon for car
Mietwagen hire car (**mieten** = to hire or rent)
and also **Wohnwagen** caravan (**wohnen** = to live in a place)

Two-wheelers

Räder (wheels)

(See also pp 67, 68)

Fahrräder bicycles
Kräder (= **Kraftfahrräder**) official jargon for motorcycles
Mofas (= **Motorfahrräder**) motorised cycles
Zweiräder two-wheelers (**zwei** = two)

Street parking

Look for the P symbol. Sometimes you must park on, or partially on, the pavement .

Anfang beginning
(of parking zone)

Some street parking is metered. Parking is usually charged in units of 30 minutes, in busy areas in units of 10 or 20 minutes. You need 10-pfennig coins.

Höchstparkzeit maximum stay
Geldeinwurf insert money

In some towns you have to use a parking disc (**Parkscheibe**). You set your time of arrival (**Ankunftzeit**) and display the disc inside the windscreen. Disc parking is usually limited to 2 hours (**2 Stunden** or **2 Std.**). You can buy discs from stationer's and other shops in the area where discs are in use.

Don't park. . .

* where it says **parken verboten** or **Fahrzeuge abstellen verboten**

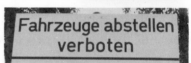

* in front of entrances and exits; you usually see **Einfahrt freihalten** or **Ausfahrt freihalten**, and sometimes both!

freihalten keep clear

* where parking is restricted to certain types of vehicle (see p 27) or to certain users, e.g. **Gäste** (guests), **Besucher** (vistors), **Kunden** (customers), and you're not among the 'privileged'. Look for **frei, nur, nur für** or **ausgenommen**.

28

* where you see a 'no stopping' or 'no waiting' sign; some state when waiting is prohibited

Ladebucht loading bay

* where you see this long-winded sign or a similar one

Illegally parked vehicles will be removed at owner's expense

It's no mere threat — you may also incur a fine!

Coping with car parks

Parkplatz is generally an open-air car park, sometimes attended (**bewacht**). You pay if you see **Gebühr**, **Parkgebühr(en)**, **gebührenpflichtig** *but* **Parkplätze** usually means parking spaces.

A multi-storey car park can be called **Parkgarage**, **Parkhaus**, **Parkhochhaus**, or if it's underground **Tiefgarage**.

Check if there's a sign outside saying **besetzt** (full) or **frei** (spaces) *but* **frei** here doesn't mean free of charge — that's **gebührenfrei**. As you drive in, a sign **Halt!** or **anhalten** means you must stop and take a ticket (but don't leave it in the car — see next page).

When you've parked your car look for **Ausgang** (exit for pedestrians). On your return go to **Eingang** (entrance for pedestrians) *not* **Einfahrt** — that's for cars only. To leave the car park follow the sign **Ausfahrt**.

Paying the parking fee

Find out if you have to pay at the cash desk (**Kasse**) or at a machine (**Automat**) *before* collecting the car. If you need small change for the machine, look for **Münzwechsler** or **Geldwechsler** (coin-changing machine). (See chapter 7.)

vor Abholung before collecting
zahlen pay

You pay by the hour (**jede Stunde** or **pro Stunde**).

jede each   **angefangene** begun
zuzüglich in addition

Checking on the opening times

Look for **geöffnet von** (open from), **geöffnet bis** (open until) or **Öffnungszeiten** (opening hours). (For days of the week see p 10.)

Kurzparker indicates a short-stay car park.

❓TEST YOURSELF

1 Who, or what kind of vehicle, is allowed to park here?

a  b  c

2 You're meeting someone at the airport. Which way do you turn to park?

3 Who is allowed to park alongside this 'no waiting' sign?

4 What information does this sign give you?

5 How much will it cost to park here? What do you have to do on your way in?

6 It's 5 o'clock on a Saturday afternoon. (i) Can you leave your car at any of these places? (ii) Will you have to pay?

a

b

c

7 It's 10 am on a Tuesday. (i) What do you need if you want to park here? (ii) Until what time can you stay?

8 Do either of these signs outside someone's front gate mean you mustn't park?

a  b

9 What might happen to your car here?

c Motorway driving

🔵 KEY WORDS

Autobahn
(motorway)

Autobahndreieck (intersection where motorways merge – **Dreieck** = triangle)
Autobahnkreuz (intersection where motorways cross – **Kreuz** = cross)

Rast
(rest)

indicates an area where you can stop for a rest or food:
Rastanlage (service area)
Rasthof, Raststätte (motorway inn)
Rastplatz (lay-by)

How to get onto the motorway

Look for the white on blue motorway symbol or the direction sign **Autobahn** *but* not **Autostrasse**: it's an expressway.

These signs tell you that you can reach Herrenberg and Stuttgart by motorway, Sindelfingen by ordinary road; 831 is the number of the motorway.

The small (white on blue) signs with **U** (= **Umleitung**, diversion) and a number refer to ordinary roads. These are permanently signposted routes for use when a stretch of the motorway is unusable. They eventually lead back to the motorway.

Important signs on the motorway

Stau warns you of a traffic jam ahead. **Kriechspur** indicates a slow lane for heavy vehicles, caravans etc. **Richtgeschwindigkeit** gives an advisory speed limit. In general there are no speed limits on motorways but you may at times be asked not to exceed a certain speed e.g. 130 kilometres (approximately 80 mph).

schneller faster
als than

Advance warnings of intersections will either say **Autobahnkreuz** or **Autobahndreieck**. They are usually named after the nearest town.

6 = number of motorway
E12 = number of long-distance route across Europe (**Europastrasse**) (white on green)

Signs like this one show you how you can tune to the local motoring service.

SDR = **Süddeutscher Rundfunk** South German Radio
UKW VHF
MW medium wave

If you want to rest or eat

Look for **Rastplatz**, signposted well in advance. Some lay-bys have tables and benches, some have toilet facilities. (See also chapter 12, p 88.)

sauber halten keep clean

If you need a service area or a restaurant look for **Rastanlage**, **Rasthaus**, **Rasthof** or **Raststätte**. They are open for essential services and food 24 hours a day (**Rund-um Service**). Some also have overnight accommodation.

Grenze frontier

. . . or get petrol

Look for a service area or **Tankstelle** (petrol station). (See also p 36.)

If you want to leave the motorway

Exits are not numbered. Instead they give the name of the nearest town they lead to. There may be several exits to one town, identified as **Nord** (north), **Süd** (south), **Mitte** (centre), **Ost** (east), **West** (west).

Ausfahrt marks the motorway exit.

If you break down

There is an orange-coloured emergency phone (**Notruf**) every two kilometres. The arrow on the black and white posts beside the hard shoulder points to the nearest phone. A beam of light marks the phone at night.

Lift flap (**Klappe**) and hold. Wait until motorway control point at Heimsheim replies.

❷ TEST YOURSELF

1 You're looking for the motorway. Which sign would lead you there?

a  b  c

2 What information do these signs provide?

a  b  c

3 You want to stop and rest. (i) Could you follow either sign? (ii) What is the difference between them?

a  b

d Going to a service station

👤 KEY WORDS

. . .dien. . . (dienen, to serve)	**Bedienung** (service − by a person) **Dienst** (service − by a firm), e.g. **Reifendienst** (tyre service)
tanken (to fill with petrol)	has to do with petrol stations and pumps: **Münztank** (coin-operated pump − **Münze** = coin) **selbsttanken, sb-tanken** for short (to fill up the tank yourself − **selbst** = self) **Tankstelle** (petrol station)

OTHER IMPORTANT WORDS

Benzin (petrol) **Öl** (oil) **Luft** (air) **Wasser** (water)

Finding a service station

There are in general plenty of petrol stations. You'll recognise self-service stations by the sign **selbsttanken**, **sb-tanken**, **sb-Tank** or simply **sb**.
but don't be misled by **sb** on its own – it isn't a brand of petrol.

On a motorway look out for **Tankstelle** or before you get on it for **Letzte Tankstelle vor der Autobahn** (last petrol station before the motorway).

Filling up the tank

There are two grades of petrol roughly equivalent to four-star and two-star.
∗ ∗ ∗ ∗ is **Super**; ∗ ∗ is called **Normal** or **Benzin** (also the word for petrol) or it's known by its brand name. You buy petrol by the litre (4.5 litres = 1 gallon), and in units of 10, 20 marks etc. unless you're filling up.
If you want to be served look for **Bedienung**.

Self-service prices are usually lower.

Geld money   **sparen** save

Self-service pumps

The operating instructions look formidable but most pumps work more or less as in Britain, except they often dispense the bill as well. It may say **Beleg** or **Tankbeleg entnehmen** (remove bill). You pay (**bezahlen**) at the cash desk (**an der Kasse**).

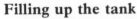

Beleg entnehmen
An der Kasse bezahlen

Coin-operated pumps

These are labelled **Münztank** and are for use when the garage is closed. To operate them you need 2- or 5-mark pieces.

Oil, air, water

Ölwechsel means you can have your oil changed. If you want it checked look for **prüfen** (check).

Is your oil level correct? We'll check immediately

For air for your tyres look for **Luft**. Tyre pressure is measured in **atü** (**1 atü** = 14.7 lbs per sq. inch).

let air out

check

put air in

For water look for **Wasser**.

Car wash

A car wash is **Autowäsche**, a quick wash **Schnellwäsche**.

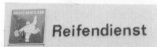

Repairs

You may get help at a service station if you have a puncture

or if the exhaust (**Auspuff**) needs attention.

But if you need a repair workshop make for **Auto-Reparaturwerkstätte**, *not* **Garage** – that's only for parking your car.

❓TEST YOURSELF

1 What does this advert tell you?

2 What takes five minutes?

3 Which sign do you look for if (i) your radiator wants topping up, (ii) your tyres need checking, (iii) you're low on petrol?

b

c

a

d

4 You've filled up with petrol. Where will you find the bill?

5 Can this service station help if (i) your battery is flat, (ii) you want your car washed, (iii) you need a tyre repaired?

Innocent abroad

38

3 LOCAL TRANSPORT (See also next chapter.)

🔑 KEY WORDS

Aus. . . (out)	**Ausgang** (way out – e.g. in stations) **Ausstieg** (exit door – in trams and buses)
Bahn (train, railway)	has to do with local and long-distance transport: **Bahnbus** (bus service run by German railways) **S-Bahn**, short for **Stadtbahn** or **Schnellbahn** (suburban line) **Strassenbahn** or **Tram** short for **Trambahn** (tram) **U-Bahn**, short for **Untergrundbahn** (underground) **U-Bahnhof, U-Bhf** (underground station) *but* **Autobahn** (motorway)
Ein. . . (in)	**einsteigen** (to board) – usually you see **nicht** **einsteigen** (do not board) **Einstieg** (entrance – to trams and buses)
Fahr. . . (**fahren**, to travel)	has to do with making a journey: **Fahrausweis, Fahrkarte, Fahrschein** (ticket) **Fahrer** (driver) **Fahrkartenschalter, Fahrkartenverkauf** (ticket office) **Fahrplan** (timetable) **Fahrpreis** (fare) **Fahrt** (journey) **Fahrzeug** (vehicle)
Karte (ticket)	what comes before it gives you the type of ticket: **Einzelfahrkarte** (ticket for one journey) **Fahrkarte** (travel ticket) **Mehrfahrtenkarte, Sammelkarte, Streifenkarte** (book or strip of tickets)

SYMBOLS WORTH KNOWING

for a bus stop. **H** = **Haltestelle** (stop).
(green on yellow)

for a tram stop; many towns have trams.
(green on yellow)

for an underground station.
(white on blue)

for a suburban line station.
(white on green)

Buying a ticket

Local transport systems and fare structures vary from place to place. As a rule, bus, tram, underground and suburban line tickets are interchangeable within the same town. Buying a book or strip of tickets (**Mehrfahrten-**, **Sammel-**, or **Streifenkarte**) can save you money.

Automat machine

For a bus or tram

It's normal to get your ticket beforehand, from a machine at the stop or sometimes from nearby kiosks and shops. Look for signs like this one.

Usually you can also buy your ticket from the driver (**Fahrer**), except where it says **im Fahrzeug kein Verkauf** (**Verkauf** = sale).

Stadtwerke municipal services
Verkehrsbetriebe transport system

For the underground or suburban line

You buy your ticket from a machine with complicated instructions by pressing a series of keys (**eintasten** or **Taste drücken**). Instructions differ considerably from town to town, but in general say something like this:

1 Select fare
2 Put in money
3 Take ticket
Cancel ticket

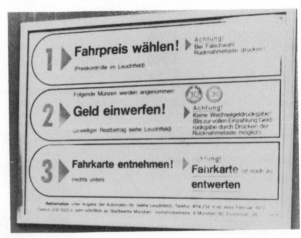

Where you see **Kein Wechselgeld zurück** or **Keine Wechselgeldrückgabe** (no change given) you should put in the exact amount (**Geld** = money, **Rückgabe** = return).

You can usually get small change from a nearby coin-changing machine (**Münzwechsler** or **Geldwechsler** – see chapter 7).

Cancelling your ticket

A bus, tram or train ticket is only valid (**gültig**) if you cancel it (**entwerten**). Look for a box marked **E** short for **Entwerter** (cancelling machine) near the ticket machine or in a bus or tram.

In some towns you stamp (**abstempeln**) your ticket in this sort of machine.

Travelling with an uncancelled ticket can mean a substantial fine.

Fahrausweis bitte hier abstempeln

Travelling in the right direction

To make sure, look for **Richtung**: it gives you the general direction, e.g. **Richtung Zoo** means 'all stations to the zoo' (and often beyond).
On stations and major tram stops an indicator board will show which platform (**Gleis**) your train (**Zug**) or tram will leave from.

S3 name of route
Maisach name of terminus
Hauptbahnhof main station

Getting on and off

Doors on underground and suburban trains open and close automatically unless there is a sign **Knopf drücken** (press button). If you want to get on a bus or tram look for the word **Einstieg**. To get off look for **Ausstieg**.

It's usual to board a bus at the front (**vorne**) and to get off at the back (**hinten**).

Einstieg bitte Knopf drücken

? TEST YOURSELF

1 What sort of stops are these?

a

b

41

2 You've arrived at the station. What public transport is available
  a at this one?   **b** And at that one?

3 You see this sign at a bus stop. What does it tell you?

4 What types of ticket can you get from these machines?

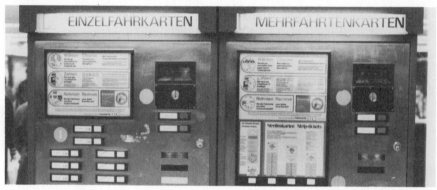

5 What is the gist of this sign?

Innocent abroad

THEY GIVE YOUR MONEY **BACK** HERE? I APPROVE OF THAT!

4 GOING BY TRAIN (See also chapter 3.)

KEY WORDS

Bahn
(train)

here short for **Eisenbahn** (railway); has to do with train travel:
Bahnhof, Bhf, Bf (station)
Bahnhof(s)gaststätte (station restaurant)
Bahnsteig (platform)
Deutsche Bundesbahn or **DB** (German Federal Railway)
Hauptbahnhof, Hbf (main station)
but **Autobahn** (motorway)

Fahr. . .
(**fahren**, to travel)

is mainly connected with travel times and tickets:
Abfahrt (departure)
Fahrkarte, Fahrschein (ticket)
Fahrkartenausgabe, Fahrkartenschalter (ticket office)

Gepäck
(luggage)

Gepäckannahme (left luggage counter)
Gepäckausgabe (counter for collecting left luggage)
Reisegepäck (heavy luggage)

Karte
(ticket)

what comes before it tells you what type of ticket:
Bahnsteigkarte (platform ticket)
Fahrkarte (travel ticket)
Platzkarte (seat reservation)

Reise
(journey)

Reiseauskunft (travel information)
Reisebüro (travel agency)
Reiseproviant (food for the journey)

Wagen
(carriage)

what comes before it tells you what type of carriage:
Liegewagen (couchette car)
Schlafwagen (sleeping car)
Speisewagen (restaurant car)
but **Kinderwagen** (pram)

Zug
(train)

has to do with specific trains and anything relating to them:
Autoreisezug (motorail)
Eilzug (semi-fast train)
Schnellzug (fast train)
Zugauskunft (train information)

OTHER IMPORTANT WORDS

Gleis (platform)   **Richtung** (direction)

Finding out about train times

Study the arrival board, marked **Ankunft**, or the departure board, marked **Abfahrt**.

Places where you can get information have a sign ⓘ, **Auskunft**, **Reiseauskunft** or **Zugauskunft**.

On big stations there are machines labelled **Reisezugauskunft**; to get the information you want, you press a series of buttons — not easy even if you know the language well.

Different types of train

IC is an Intercity train, **TEE** a Trans-Europe Express. To travel on them you have to pay a special supplement (**Sonderzuschlag**). Some trains are named — for example **Gambrinus**, **Hans Sachs**.

E on the indicator board or timetable stands for **Eilzug**.
D is the symbol for **D-Zug** or **Schnellzug**.

Buying a ticket

Go to the counter marked **Fahrkarten**, **Fahrkartenausgabe** or **Fahrkartenschalter**. There may be several counters. For travel inside Germany go to the one with **Inland** on it; for travel outside Germany it should say **Ausland**. But if you're travelling to East Germany, look for the counter marked **DDR Verkehr**. For seat reservations find the counter **Platzkarten**.

You can also buy rail tickets from travel agents with this sign.

amtlicher official
Verkauf sale
DER = Deutsches Reisebüro

Coping with luggage

On most stations there are trolleys (**Kofferkulis**). To leave your luggage look for **Gepäckannahme**, but remember to collect it from **Gepäckausgabe**. If you prefer luggage lockers pick out the sign **Schliessfächer**. A locker with a green sign **frei** is empty, with a red one **belegt** is not.

Instructions

1 open door, put in luggage, close door
2 insert money
3 press against door and lock it
4 take out key note locker number

Finding the platform and boarding the train

Signs like these direct you to the platform and the trains.

Richtung before a place name gives you the direction the train is going in. On the platform you'll find an indicator board with train details (see page 44) and a plan showing the order of the carriages (**Wagenstandanzeiger**). If you want to smoke look for a carriage marked **Raucher** (white on red), otherwise **Nichtraucher**.

Facilities at stations

Warteraum or **Wartesaal** is a waiting room.
If you want a meal, look for . . .**gaststätte** or . . .**restaurant**.

Places where you can go for a snack are indicated by **Erfrischungen** (refreshments), **Imbiss** or **Kaltes Buffet**.
Reiseproviant tells you that you can get food to take on the journey.

kaltes cold

At many stations you can buy souvenirs (**Andenken**), flowers (**Blumen**), sweets (**Süsswaren**), tobacco and cigarettes (**Tabak** or **Tabakwaren**), and newspapers and magazines (**Zeitschriften**).

You can change money at main stations at a **Wechselstube** (see p 56).
To get help with finding accommodation look for **Zimmernachweis** (see next chapter).

❓ TEST YOURSELF

1 Why isn't this the right counter for train information?

2 Which word tells you that you can make your motorail booking here?

3 Which of these will you follow if you want to leave your luggage?

a

b

c

4 Where does this sign direct you to?

5 You're looking for the waiting room. Is this sign any help?

6 At which of these counters can you (i) buy a ticket to London (ii) reserve a seat?

b

a

7 What facilities are available at this station?

8 This way if you want to send goods express. What else?

Innocent abroad

'KINDER' ARE CHILDREN AREN'T THEY? I'M NOT TRAVELLING IN A CARRIAGE FULL OF KIDS!

Kinderwagen und Traglasten

5 ACCOMMODATION

KEY WORDS

Fremde
(strangers)

Fremdenheim (hostel)
Fremdenverkehrsverein (tourist office)
Fremdenzimmer (room/s to let)

Gast
(guest)

can refer to people staying in a hotel, campsite etc. or to the accommodation itself:
Gasthaus, Gasthof (inn)
Gästehaus (guest house)
Gästezimmer (guest room/s)
Campinggäste (campers)
Hotelgäste (hotel guests)
but **Gaststätte** is a restaurant without accommodation

Zimmer
(room)

Gästezimmer (see **Gast** above)
Zimmernachweis, Zimmervermittlung (accommodation bureau)

OTHER IMPORTANT WORDS

frei (available)   **belegt** or **besetzt** (full)

Finding accommodation

To save you the trouble of finding rooms yourself look for the accommodation bureau (**Zimmernachweis** or **Zimmervermittlung**). There may be one at the station, in the town centre or in the **Verkehrsbüro** or **Verkehrsamt** (tourist office). (See also p 59.) You'll be charged a nominal fee for the booking. If you prefer to find your own accommodation and want something other than the conventional hotel look for **Hotel Garni** (bed and breakfast hotel), **Pension** (boarding house), **Gästehaus** or **Fremdenheim**.

If you want to stay at an inn (**Gasthaus** or **Gasthof**) or in a private house, watch out for the signs **Zimmer, Gästezimmer, Fremdenzimmer** or **Zimmer frei**. There's no point in enquiring further if it says **besetzt** or **belegt**.

Note: **Hof** can be short for **Gasthof** – or it can indicate a very superior type of hotel.

If you're youth-hostelling look for a sign with **Jugendherberge** (youth-hostel) or with **DJH** = **Deutsches Jugendherbergswerk** (German Youth Hostel Association).

You'll recognise holiday flats by this sign.

If you want overnight accommodation when travelling on the motorway look for a motel or a motorway inn (**Raststätte**).

Amenities you may be offered

Some signs for private rooms tell you what amenities there are, for example a bath (**Bad**),

or running water (**fliessendes Wasser**), or even central heating (**Zentralheizung**).

fl. = **fliessendes** running
kalt cold

Booking in

In a hotel or inn look for **Rezeption** or **Empfang** (reception).

Kasse cashier

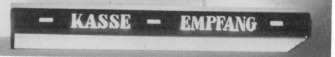

Elsewhere it's **Anmeldung** or **anmelden**.

Staying at a camp site

Charges and camp rules are displayed at the entrance.

Charges for overnight stay
Adults
Young people
Children 2—14 years old
Caravan or tent
Car
Motor cycle with tent (pitch)
Electricity

ÜBERNACHTUNGS-GEBÜHREN	
Erwachsene	3.-
Jugendliche	2.-
Kinder 2 - 14 Jahre	1.50
Wohnwagen oder Zelt	2.-
Auto	2.-
Motorrad mit Zelt (Stellplatz)	3.-
Strom	2.-

Regulations are strict, and there are many do's and don't's.

Ruhe quiet   **laute** loud

There is also a quiet period in the afternoon (**Mittagsruhe**) when you can't even use your car.

während during
Durchfahrt way through (for vehicles)

Arrangements for rubbish disposal, washing up (**abwaschen**) etc. are clearly signposted.

Abfälle rubbish
Abfallbehälter rubbish disposal bag

Most camp sites have electricity (**Strom**) for the use of campers. There is usually a self-service shop (**Selbstbedienungsladen** or **SB Laden** for short) and often a restaurant (**Gaststätte**).

Geschirr crockery

❓ TEST YOURSELF

1 Where is the accommodation office in this town?

2 This is a hotel with a difference. Why?

3 If you were looking for a room, which of these signs would you follow up?

a

b

4 Who can use this entrance?

Zutritt nur für Campinggäste

5 Is this a warning or a prohibition sign? What does it say about crockery?

Geschirr abwaschen untersagt!

6 Why is your attention drawn to these times?

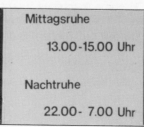

6 AT THE POST OFFICE

This is the post office symbol (black on yellow, the official post office colours)

🔵 KEY WORDS

Brief (letter)	has to do with posting a letter: **Briefeinwurf** (slot for posting letters) **Briefkasten** (letter box) **Briefmarke** (stamp)
Fern. . . (long-distance)	relates to telecommunications: **Ferngespräch** (long-distance call) **Fernsprecher** (official word for 'telephone')
Post (post, post office)	**Deutsche Bundespost** or **DBP** (German Federal Post Office) **Postamt** (post office) **postlagernd** ('poste restante') **Postwertzeichen** (official word for 'postage stamp')
Ruf (call)	**Notruf** (emergency call) **Rufnummer** (telephone number)

Buying stamps

At the post office (**Post** or **Postamt**) look for the counter marked **Briefmarken** or **Postwertzeichen**.

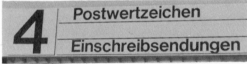

Einschreibsendungen registered mail

In large post offices, **in kleinen Mengen** or **kl.Mengen** (small amounts) is often added. This is the counter to go to if you only need a few stamps. Stamp collectors should look for the counter **Sondermarken** (commemorative stamps).

There are also stamp machines outside most post offices.
On some machines, you turn a handle and lift a flap for the stamps, on others you pull out (**ziehen**) a drawer.

This tells you what coins to insert.

If the machine doesn't work, press button (**Knopf drücken**). You get your money back.

Look here for rejected coins.

If you haven't the right change try to find a coin-changing machine (**Münzwechsler**). There's usually one near a stamp machine. (For details see p.57.)

You can also get stamps from a newsagent or kiosk provided you buy your postcards (**Postkarten**) there.

Posting a letter or a parcel

Some post boxes with frequent collections have a large red dot.

Most boxes give details of the next collection (**nächste Leerung**) and days and times of other collections. They often tell you where to find the nearest box with a late-night collection (**Nachtleerung**).

To post a parcel (**Paket**) take it to **Paketannahme**. **Paketausgabe** is where you collect parcels.

Making a phone call

From a public box

A black-on-yellow sign on a call box merely confirms that it's a public telephone.

öffentlicher public

A black-on-green sign means you can make calls to anywhere inside Germany (**Inlandsgespräche**) or abroad (**Auslandsgespräche**). Some of these boxes are now marked **National u.International**.

The minimum charge – also the price of a timed local call – is 20 pfennigs, i.e. usually you need to have two **10-Pfennig** coins to operate a public telephone.

If you have to insert more money during a call a light will come on saying **Bitte zahlen** (please pay).

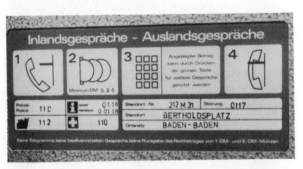

You can call the police or fire brigade without using coins from a phone box marked **Münzfreier Notruf**. (See chapter 14 p 95.)

From the post office

There are coin-operated call boxes inside most post offices. For a long-distance call you may prefer to go to the counter **Ferngespräche**. You will be allocated a phone box which you don't need to feed with coins; you pay at the counter when you have finished telephoning.

❓TEST YOURSELF

1 When will your letter be collected?

NÄCHSTE LEERUNG

MONTAG

10 Uhr

2 You want to (i) send a telegram
(ii) buy stamps for your collection
(iii) post a parcel. Which of these
can you do at this counter?

1 Postwertzeichen
Sondermarken
Wert-und Einschreibsendungen
Ferngespräche Telegramme
Briefausgabe
Wechselsteuermarken

3 Which counter would you make for
if you wanted to (i) make a phone
call (ii) buy a couple of stamps (iii)
pick up your 'poste restante' mail
(iv) send a registered letter?

2 Postlagernde Sendungen
Postwertzeichen kl. Mengen
Wert - Einschreibsendungen

6 Einzahlungen Ausland
Postsparkasse
Postbarscheckauszahlungen

11 Telegramme
Ferngespräche

4 When should you press this button
on a stamp machine?

Bei Versagen
Knopf drücken

5 What's so special
about these two?

a

BRIEFE

b

Münzfreier Notruf

Innocent abroad

IT MUST BE
THE WAY TO
YE OLDE
POST OFFICE!

Gasthof zur Post

7 COPING WITH MONEY

👤 KEY WORDS

Einwurf
(slot)

has to do with putting coins into a machine:
einwerfen (to insert coins)
Geldeinwurf (place for putting in money)
Münzeinwurf (coin slot – **Münze** = coin)

Geld
(money)

see **Einwurf** above and **Wechsel** below

Kasse
(cashier's, cash desk)

Sparkasse (savings bank)

Schalter
(counter)

Auslandsschalter (foreign counter)
Autoschalter (drive-in counter)
Schalterstunden, Schalterzeiten (banking hours)

Wechsel
(change)

helps you to identify a place or machine where you
can change money:
Geldwechsel, Wechselstube (exchange bureau)
Geldwechsler, Münzwechsler (coin-changing machine)
Wechselgeld (small change)
but **Wechsel** is also the word for 'bill of exchange'

Where you can change money

* At almost any **Bank**

   but don't be misled by **Spielbank**: it
   means 'casino' (**spielen** = to play or
   gamble), or by **Wechselbank** – that's a
   finance company.

* At a savings bank (**Sparkasse**).

* At airports: look for
   the sign **Geldwechsel**.

Stadt town

* At main railway stations:
   the exchange bureau is
   called **Wechselstube**.

Aktiengesellschaft joint-stock company

Banking hours

Banks are open Mondays to Fridays in the mornings and afternoons, with late closing on Thursdays. Beware: banks close at lunchtime.
(Check days of the week on p 10)

At airports and big railway stations you can also change money at weekends and often until late at night.

Counters to look for in a bank

If you want to change money and there is no notice saying 'Change' or 'Exchange', look for **Reiseverkehr** (foreign travel), **Auslandsschalter** (foreign counter), **Geldwechsel** (money exchange), **Devisen** (foreign or travellers' cheques) or **Sorten** (foreign currency).

At the end of the transaction you may have to collect your money from the cashier (**Kasse**).

Operating a coin-changing machine

You may need small change (**Kleingeld**) for a stamp machine, a parking meter or other type of machine. There is often a coin-changing machine (**Münzwechsler** or **Geldwechsler**) nearby.

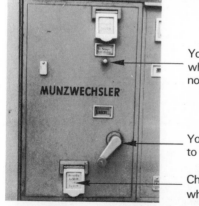

You use this button when the machine does not work. (See p 53.)

Rückgabe change given

You turn the handle to get the change.

Change given here where it says **Ausgabe**.

Beware: when you put coins into a machine, particularly for parking fees, make sure it's the exact amount where you see **kein Wechselgeld zurück** (no change given).

❷ TEST YOURSELF

1 You want to change travellers cheques. Which of these would you go to?

a  **SPIELBANK**   b **DRESDNER BANK**

2 It's five o'clock on a Thursday afternoon. Is this bank still open?

yes

Schalterzeiten
Montag – Freitag 8-12 u. 14-16 Uhr
Donnerstag verlängert
bis 18 Uhr

3 (i) Would you go to change money at this counter?

SCHECK – WECHSEL

(ii) Or would you make for the 'quick service' counter?

Schnellservice
nur Annahme
keine Beratung
Geldwechsel

4 What do you get here?

MÜNZWECHSLER

5 What do you have to do here?

1.– DM
Münzeinwurf

Innocent abroad

IS THE 'FUNDBÜRO' THE OFFICE TO GO TO WHEN YOU RUN OUT OF **FUNDS**?

**Kasse
Fundbüro** ▶

8 SIGHTSEEING (See also chapter 9.)

🔑 KEY WORDS

Eintritt (admission)	**Eintrittskarte** (admission ticket) **Eintrittspreis** (admission charge)
Fahrt (trip, journey)	can describe a trip or sightseeing tour: **Alpenfahrt** (tour of the Alps) **Rückfahrt** (return journey) **Rundfahrt** (round trip) **Sonderfahrt** (special tour) *but* **Abfahrt** tells you the time and place of departure **Ausfahrt, Einfahrt, Vorfahrt** etc. have to do with motoring (see p 20).
Karte (ticket)	what comes before it tells you what type of ticket: **Eintrittskarte** (see **Eintritt** above) **ermässigte Karte** (reduced ticket) **Fahrkarte** (travel ticket) **Tageskarte** (day ticket)
Rund. . . (round)	means coming back to your starting point: **Rundfahrt** (see **Fahrt** above) **Rundgang** (way round a particular place) **Rundweg** (path round a particular area)
Stadt (town)	**Altstadt** (old part of the town) **Innenstadt, Stadtmitte** (town centre) **städtisch** (municipal)
Zeit (time)	**Besichtigungszeiten** (visiting times) **Fahrzeit** (travelling time) **Öffnungszeiten** (opening hours)

To find out what there is to see

Look for **Verkehrsamt, Verkehrsbüro, Verkehrsverein** or **Fremdenverkehrsverein** (tourist office). You may sometimes have to pay a small charge for their maps, brochures etc.

In a spa (**Kurort**) the **Kurverwaltung** (spa office) gives the same service.

Spielbank casino

Large railway stations, town centres etc. have tourist information offices marked **🛈** or **Auskunft** (information).

Taking a trip

For organised sightseeing look for **Reisebüro** (travel agency). An excursion or tour may be advertised as **Ausflug** or **Fahrt**.

Omnibus bus, coach

To find the time or place of departure look for **ab** or **Abfahrt**; for the time of return **zurück** or **Rückfahrt**; for the time of arrival **an**; for the destination **nach**.

grosse big   **Bodensee** Lake Constance
Schweiz Switzerland

To find out what a trip costs look for **Fahrpreis** (cost of journey) or **Hin- und Rückfahrt** (return). On a mountain railway check if the **Bergfahrt** (ride up) costs more than the **Talfahrt** (ride down).
Booking offices may be marked **Fahrkarten**, **Fahrkartenschalter** or just **Schalter** (ticket counter), or **Kasse** (cash desk). Sometimes you have to buy your ticket on the bus, boat etc.

nächste next   **Schiff** boat

Sightseeing in town

An organised tour of the town is **Stadtrundfahrt**. If you want to explore the town centre for yourself look for **Innenstadt** or **Stadtmitte**.

Kurhaus pump-room in a spa

Altstadt points the way to the old part of the town, usually with interesting old streets. It may be worth looking for signs with **Stadtmauer** (town wall), . . .**burg** (castle), . . .**tor** (gate) or . . .**turm** (tower) or signs directing you to buildings like the **Rathaus** (town hall).

Looking at churches

A church (**Kirche**) of special interest is often signposted: for example **Wallfahrtskirche** (church to which pilgrimages are made), **Klosterkirche** (monastery church). Other churches worth visiting are **Dom** (cathedral), **Münster** (minster), **Abtei** (abbey) and **Kapelle** (chapel).

Church signs at the edge of towns will tell you the days and times of services; if the church is named it's probably one you should go and see.

Heilige Messe Holy Mass

Looking at castles and palaces

Burg is usually a medieval castle, occasionally a palace. Towns called . . .**burg**, for example **Hamburg**, were built around a castle, although the castle may have disappeared.

Schloss is the name for a large country house, palace or castle; the grounds (**Schlossgarten** or **Schlosspark**) are often worth a visit. A summer palace is sometimes called **Lustschloss** (**Lust** means pleasure not lust!).
If you want to know how old a place is look for **erbaut** (built) or **Jahrhundert** (century), sometimes shortened to **Jahrh**.

To find out more about the place you're visiting see if there's a **Führung** (guided tour) or a **Führer** (guide or guide book).

besuchen Sie visit
älteste oldest

Visiting museums and exhibitions

In addition to the big national museums (e.g. **Deutsches Museum** in Munich), you'll find many small museums. Practically every town has a **Heimatmuseum** (local history museum). **Landesmuseum** means it belongs to a **Land** (one of the German Federal States).

Monat month

A display within a museum is called **Sammlung** (collection); **Ausstellung** is an exhibition.

Sonder. . . special

Most museums are closed on a Monday (**Montag**).

Visiting parks, gardens and zoos

Look out for **Garten** (garden) or **Park**,
e.g. **Botanischer Garten, Kurgarten** or
Kurpark (in a spa).
Tiergarten or **Tierpark** is a zoo
but **Kindergarten** is a nursery school, not
a garden or playground for children.

The official word for both parks and
gardens you see on many notices is
Anlage.

Times when places are open

Look for **Öffnungszeiten, Besichtigung** or
Besichtigungszeiten

or for **geöffnet** or **geschlossen** with **ab**
or **von** (from).

Watch out for **Kassenschluss**: it tells you
when the ticket office or cash desk
closes, i.e. the time of the last
admission.

sind are

Getting a ticket

The ticket office is marked **Eintritt,
Eintrittskarten, Eintrittspreise, Kasse,** or
sometimes **Kartenverkauf** (sale of
tickets). If you're 16 or over, you
generally pay the rate for **Erwachsene**
(adults). Children under 6 are often free
(**frei**). There may be reduced rates for:
* 6—15 year olds: **Kinder ab** or **von 6
  Jahren, Schüler** (pupils)
* over 65s: **Personen ab 65 Jahren,
  Senioren, Rentner** (pensioners)
* families (**Familien**), parties (**Gruppen**),
  students (**Studenten** or **Schüler ab
  16 Jahren**)

To qualify for a reduction (**Ermässigung**)
you may be asked for proof; a German
would produce his identity card
(**Ausweis**).

Doppelkarte double ticket
Lustheim name of palace
neues new
wie oben as above

Exploring the countryside

Tourist routes of scenic, historical or architectural interest are marked
. . .**strasse**, e.g.
Schwarzwaldhochstrasse (Black Forest mountain route), **Romantische Strasse** (Romantic route), **Alpenstrasse** (Alpine route). Each route has its own colour code and symbol.

To find places of scenic interest look for signs with
. . .**see** (lake)
. . .**tal** (valley), e.g. **Rheintal**
. . .**höhle** (cave)

Bären bears

or . . .**schutzgebiet** (protected area), e.g.
Naturschutzgebiet (nature reserve) and
Landschaftsschutzgebiet (conservation area).

but **Wasserschutzgebiet** (protected water area) is a warning to tanker drivers not to pollute water supplies!

If you want to get up a mountain the easy way look for . . .**bahn** (railway) —
Bergbahn (mountain railway), **Seilbahn** or **Gondelbahn** (cable railway).

fahr travel
Dürkheim place name

Don't ignore signs saying **Aussicht** or **Aussichtspunkt**, **Blick** or **Ausblick** — they take you to places where you get a good view. Sometimes there's an **Aussichtsturm** (look-out tower).

schönste most beautiful **über** over

Joining in local festivities

Look for posters advertising . . .**fest** (festival or fête). Festivals usually last several days, with sideshows, dancing and plenty of beer and wine. Nearly every village or community has its **Schützenfest** (rifle club festival) or **Volksfest** (people's festival). Towns and villages in wine-growing areas have their own special festivals – **Weinfest**, **Weinlesefest** or **Winzerfest**.

but **Schlachtfest** ('slaughter festival') which you may see advertised in village butcher's shops and inns means that an animal, usually a pig, has just been slaughtered and fresh meat delicacies are available.

heute today

❓ TEST YOURSELF

1 If you're sightseeing which signs should you follow?

2 What would you expect to find if you went this way?

a

b

3 You'd like to get a good view of Munich's Olympic Park. Which of these should you make for?

4 Where does this sign point to?

5 You want to take a boat trip. Where do you get a ticket?

a
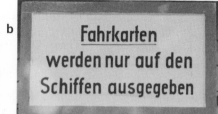

b

6 What are you being encouraged to do? What does the second line tell you about the place?

7 Your family consists of 2 adults, a 12-year-old and a 16-year-old college student. What will be the total cost of admission?

8 On what days can you visit this museum? Even if you can't make out every word, what special things can you see there?

9 OUT IN THE OPEN

Walking (See also chapter 8.)

🔒 KEY WORDS

Pfad
(path)

often describes a path laid out for a special purpose or along a particular route:
Trimm-Dich-Pfad, **Waldsportpfad** (path with keep-fit equipment)
Weinpfad (path through wine-growing areas)

Wald
(forest, woodland)

occurs in place names, e.g. **Schwarzwald** (Black Forest), or indicates a wooded area:
Waldparkplatz (woodland car park)
Waldweg (woodland path)

Wander. . .
(**wandern**, to hike)

words beginning with **Wander. . .** should interest hikers:
Wanderkarte (map showing footpaths)
Wanderparkplatz ('park-and-hike' car park)
Wanderweg (marked footpath)

Weg
(way, path)

what comes before it tells you what type of path:
Fussweg (footpath)
Rundweg, **Rundwanderweg** (path around an area)

How to discover good walks

In areas of scenic beauty there is usually a network of well signposted footpaths (**Wanderwege**). Outside railway stations, in village and town centres, or at a bus terminus there may be a sign labelled **Wandertafel** listing attractive walks.

> ### WANDERWEGE
> #### OrtenauerWeinpfad Baden-Baden-Offenburg
> ##### Beginn: Obushaltestelle „Tiergarten"

Obushaltestelle = Omnibushaltestelle bus stop

Finding out where the path leads to

Some signs give the towns where the walk begins and ends. Otherwise look for **zum, zur, nach** (to) or just a place name. Long-distance footpaths generally have a name, e.g. **Ortenauer Weinpfad**. A **Rundweg** or **Rundwanderweg** often starts from a special car park for hikers (**Wanderparkplatz**) and takes you back there!

Blössling name of a hill

Note the symbol on the signpost for the route you're taking; follow it until you reach your destination.

Stadtmitte town centre

. . . and how far your destination is

Maps and signposts give distances in kilometres (**km**) or in hours (**Stunden** or **Std**) and minutes (**Minuten** or **Min**) or in 'walking time' (**Gehzeit**).

See lake

If you'd like more strenuous exercise

Look for **Waldsportpfad** or **Trimm-Dich-Pfad**, a woodland walk with keep-fit equipment and instructions on its use.

Don't go. . .

where you're asked to keep out: you'll see **nicht betreten** or **Betreten verboten**.

Betreten der Wiese verboten

Wiese meadow

Cycling

KEY WORDS

fahren
(to travel)
+
Rad
(wheel, cycle)

make up most of the words to do with cycling:
Fahrrad or **Rad** for short (bicycle)

radfahren (to cycle)
Radfahrer (cyclist)
Radweg (cycle track)

Rule of the road (See also chapter 2, p21)

Alongside many roads is a **Radweg** which you should use. It's sometimes possible to cycle on footpaths and pavements provided it doesn't interfere with pedestrians.

ausweichen to give way, i.e. to pedestrians

Radfahrer ausweichen

You can often go where cars are prohibited.
(See pp 22, 24.)

But you may not cycle in a pedestrian precinct (**Fussgängerzone**) or a shopping centre (**Einkaufszentrum** or **EKZ**), and in many places, especially parks, even pushing a bike (**radschieben**) is not allowed.

Crossing the road

At crossroads look out for separate small sets of traffic lights intended for cyclists

or for written instructions on how to cross (**überqueren**) the roadway (**Fahrbahn**).

absteigen dismount

Knopf drücken press button
Grün abwarten wait for green

'Parking' your bike

Parking signs may refer to **Zweiräder** or **Zweiradfahrzeuge** (two-wheelers) or **Zweiradfahrer** (cyclists and motorcyclists). (See also p 27.)

abstellen to leave

Look also for **Abstellplatz** (place for leaving something) and **Fahrradständer** (cycle stands).

Schülereingang pupils' entrance

Don't leave your bike where **anlehnen** (leaning against something) is forbidden.

Note: you can hire bicycles at many German railway stations.

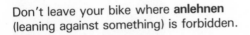

68

Going swimming

🧍 KEY WORDS

Bad
(pool, bath)

what comes before it tells you what kind of pool or bathing establishment:
Freibad (in the open air)
Hallenbad (indoors)
Schwimmbad (see **Schwimm. . .** below)
Strandbad (with a beach, on a stretch of river, lake or sea)

but **Thermalbad** is a spa treatment with hot spring water; you also see **Bad** in place names for spas, e.g. **Bad Ems, Wiesbaden.**

Bade. . .
(**baden**, to swim, bathe)

has mainly to do with bathing areas and equipment:
Badegelände, Badeplatz, Badestelle (bathing area)
Bademütze (bathing cap)
Badestrand (bathing beach)
Badeverbot (bathing prohibited)

Kleider
(clothes)

has to do with getting changed:
ankleiden (to get dressed)
auskleiden (to undress)
Kleiderablage (cloakroom)
Umkleide (changing room)

Schwimm. . .
(**schwimmen**, to swim)

Nichtschwimmer (non-swimmer/s)
Schwimmbad (general word for swimming pool)
Schwimmbecken (pool of a particular kind)
Schwimmhalle (indoor pool)

Where to swim

If you prefer an open-air pool look for **Freibad**; a heated one is **beheiztes Freibad**.

Berthold name of pool

Hallenbad or Schwimmhalle means it's indoors (**Halle** = hall).

Jugendl. = **Jugendliche** young people
Erwachsene adults

In a large complex (**Badezentrum**) you may have several pools (**Becken**). Non-swimmers look for **Nichtschwimmerbecken**. Small children might need the **Planschbecken** (paddling pool). If you can swim make for **Schwimmbecken** or **Sportbecken**. If you're keen on diving (**springen**) see if there's a **Sprungbecken**.

nördliches northern
geheizt heated

Note: **geheizt** and **beheizt** both mean 'heated'.

Paying to go in

To find out the appropriate charge see chapter 8, p 62.
In many pools the time you may spend there (**Badezeit**) is strictly limited – and includes changing. If you want to stay longer you pay extra.

einschliesslich including

Getting changed

Changing rooms can be called **Auskleide**, **Umkleide**, **Umkleideräume** or **Wechselkabinen**; **Sammelumkleide** is for communal changing. If you've paid for a single cabin, look for **Einzelkabinen**. The section for women is marked **Damen**, the one for men **Herren**.

Kleiderablage, Garderobe or Wäscheaufbewahrung are either lockers or cloakrooms for leaving your clothes.

If you want the showers look for **Duschen**.

Most pools insist that everyone (both sexes!) should wear (**tragen**) a bathing cap. Sometimes you'll see **Bademützpflicht** (bathing cap obligatory).

·Alle Badegäste
tragen beim Schwimmen
eine Bademütze !

Badegäste visitors to the pool
beim when

Bathing in ponds, lakes, rivers and the sea

This may be restricted to certain areas.
The sign will say **Badegelände**,
Badeplatz, **Badestelle** or **Badestrand**.
Don't bathe where you see **Badeverbot**.

Bachmündung
mouth of the stream

Boating

You may want to hire a boat (**Boot**).
Look for signs with **Verleih** (hire) or **zu**
vermieten (for hire). If you enjoy rowing
(**rudern**) look for **Ruderboote**; if you
want a pedal boat see if there are
Tretboote or **Velo-Boote**; for the lazy
there may be **Motorboote** (motorboats)
or **Elektroboote** (battery-powered boats).

Prices are quoted per hour (**pro Stunde,
für 1 Stunde** or **für 1 Std.**)

jede weitere
each additional

Boating is usually forbidden wherever
bathing is allowed, and vice versa.
Sometimes both are forbidden.

Somewhere for the children to play

🔑 KEY WORD

spielen   **Ballspiele** (ball games)
(to play)   **Spielplatz** (playground)

Children can't play just anywhere. You
will come across many signs forbidding
ball games and other activities.

Herz heart
Stadtverwaltung town council

So look for **Spielplatz** or **Kinderspielplatz**. But there may be restrictions on its use, for example, age limits: **unter 7 Jahren** (under seven years), **bis 14 Jahre** (up to age 14)

or its use (**Benutzung**) may be forbidden on certain days.

an Sonn-u.Feiertagen on Sundays and public holidays

❓TEST YOURSELF

1 You want to go for a long walk.
   What information do these signs give you?

a

b

c

2 You'd love a swim. Which of these signs can help you?

a

b

c

3 You're taking your 15-year-old daughter swimming. What will it cost you both to go in?

4 You've taken a single cabin. Which sign should you follow?

a  b

5 Two signs that diving enthusiasts should take note of. What do they say?

a  b

6 If you're cycling, what do you have to do here?

a  b

FAHRRÄDER
ANLEHNEN VERBOTEN,
BENUTZEN SIE BITTE
DIE FAHRRADSTÄNDER

7 What are you not supposed to do?

a

Skateboard
und Radfahren
in der Passage
verboten!

b

Wir haben einen
Badestrand und keinen
Fußballplatz –
Ball-Spielen jeder Art
verboten.
Musik unerwünscht

Innocent abroad

IT MUST BE A WARNING NOT TO OVERDO THE SUNBATHING!

Grillen im Badegelände verboten

10 SHOPS AND SERVICES

KEY WORDS

. . .dien. . . (dienen, to serve)	Words with bedien. . . have to do with self-service: bedienen Sie sich (serve yourself) Selbstbedienung, SB for short (self-service) Words with . . .dienst tell you about service by a firm: Kundendienst (customer service) Schnelldienst, Sofortdienst (quick service)
Kasse (cash desk)	Kassenzettel (receipt) Zentralkasse (main cash desk)
Kauf (purchase)	Words with Einkauf concern shopping: Einkaufskorb (basket in supermarket) Einkaufswagen (trolley in supermarket) Einkaufstip (best buy) Einkaufszentrum, EKZ for short (shopping centre) Words with Verkauf have to do with selling: Ausverkauf ('sale') Räumungsverkauf (clearance sale) Sommerschlussverkauf, SSV for short (end-of-summer sale)
Markt (market)	Marktplatz (market place) Supermarkt (supermarket)
Preis (price)	is often intended to draw your attention to a bargain: Preisaktion (special offer) Preisknüller (fabulous offer) preiswert (cheap, i.e. value for money)
Reparatur (repair)	Reparatur-Werkstatt/Werkstätte (repair workshop) repariert (repaired)
Sonder. . . (special)	Sonderangebot (special offer) Sonderpreis (special price)
Waren (goods)	Words with . . .waren describe different types of goods, or shops selling them, or departments in a store or supermarket: Fleischwaren (meat produce) Frischwaren (fresh foods, greengrocer's) Süsswaren (sweets, sweetshop) Tabakwaren (cigarettes and tobacco, tobacconist's)

KEY SENTENCE PATTERNS

wird
werden
(will be)

plus the word at the end of the sentence tell you what will or will not be done:
Jeder Diebstahl wird angezeigt (every theft will be reported, i.e. to the police = thieves will be prosecuted)
Reklamationen werden nicht anerkannt (complaints will not be accepted)

. . .en Sie

is a request to you:
kontrollieren Sie (check)
wählen Sie selbst (choose for yourself)
zahlen Sie or **bezahlen Sie** (pay)

Shop signs to look for

As a rule shops advertise their goods and services more prominently than the name of the shop. Look for words with
* . . .erei/erie e.g. **Bäckerei** (bakery)

Drogerie chemist's selling toiletries etc.

* **Geschäft** (business, shop) e.g.
  Weingeschäft (wine shop)
  Handlung (dealers) e.g. **Buchhandlung** (book shop)
  Laden (shop) e.g. **Blumenladen** (florist's)
  or **Waren** (goods) e.g. **Lederwaren** (leather goods)

Fachgeschäft specialists

* or for the things you want to buy, e.g.
  Kleider (clothes), **Schuhe** (shoes).

Bücher books   Schallplatten records

If you want souvenirs or presents

For souvenirs look for **Andenken, Reiseandenken** – for presents **Geschenke, Geschenkartikel.**
If you're invited to someone's home, the custom is to buy flowers (**Blumen**) for your hostess.

Spotting a bargain

Words with **Verkauf** often tell you that there's a sale on. **Ausverkauf, Totalausverkauf, Räumungsverkauf** are clearance sales. Sometimes the only indication of an end-of-summer sale is a sign saying **SSV (Sommerschlussverkauf)** or there may be **Sonderangebote** (special offers) or the **Angebot der Woche** (this week's offer).

Any mention of **Preis** should attract you. A 'bargain' may be advertised as **Preisaktion** or **Preisknüller**.

Shopping in department stores

Many stores include **Kauf. . .** in their name, e.g. **Kaufhof, Kaufhalle**. The different departments carry signs similar to the ones you see on shops, or they may be identified by **. . .abteilung** (department), e.g. **Sportabteilung**, or **. . .waren** e.g. **Spielwaren** (toys). If you want to exchange goods look for **Umtausch** and remember to bring your **Kassenzettel** or **Quittung** (receipt).

If you have a complaint find the customer service (**Kundendienst**).

Self-service

Selbstbedienung, Selbstbedienungsladen or **SB-Laden** tells you it's self-service. Many stores and shops have signs urging you to select what you want (**Bedienen Sie sich selbst** or **Wählen Sie selbst**) and then pay at the cash desk. Look for **Kasse**.

You'll also notice prominent signs about shoplifting. They mention **Dieb** (thief), **Diebstahl** (theft) or **Ladendieb** (shoplifter).

jeder every
wir erheben we charge

Shopping for food

Many department stores have a self-service food department. Look for **Lebensmittel** (food).

Pfannkuch name of shop

A **Supermarkt** often has a name with . . .markt, e.g. **Aldi-Markt, Edeka-Markt**. Inside you'll see many reminders to use an **Einkaufswagen** or **Einkaufskorb**.

You may prefer to go to small shops:
* for bread look for **Bäckerei** (bakery); **Bäckerei-Konditorei** or **Feinbäckerei** sells both bread and cakes

* for fresh fruit (**Obst**) and vegetables (**Gemüse**) the shop sign will probably say **Frischwaren** (greengroceries)
* for groceries the sign will read **Lebensmittel**, for specially select foods **Feinkost**

* for meat, sausage, cooked meats look for **Fleischwaren**; for a butcher's shop you'll need to recognise different words in different areas: **Metzgerei, Fleischerei** or **Schlachterei**
  but for poultry (**Geflügel**) or game (**Wild**) you may have to go to a shop that also sells fish

* for butter (**Butter**), cheese (**Käse**), eggs (**Eier**), milk (**Milch**) look for **Molkerei** (dairy). Milk (which is not delivered to homes) is generally long-life (**haltbare** or **H-Milch**)

* for special foods find a health food shop (**Reformhaus** — nothing to do with reform); an **Apotheke** (chemist's) also sells foods for special diets (**Diätwaren**)

* for alcoholic drinks look for **Weine, Spirituosen** (spirits), **Weinhaus** or **Weinverkauf. Getränke** (drinks) usually means soft drinks and beer. Note: there are no licensing hours!

Finding out what you get for your money

(See also prices p 11)

Fresh foods are priced and sold
* by the kilogram: look for **Kilo** or **kg**.

* by the pound: look for **Pfund, Pfd.** or
  ℔, or for ½ **Kilo**, ½ **kg**. or
  500 **Gramm** (English pound = 454g)

* in units of grams: look for **50g, 100g,**
  250g etc. (**g** = **Gramm**)

> **echter** real
> **Allgäuer Emmenthaler** cheese from the
> Allgäu region

* singly: look for **Stück** or **St.** or **je, jede**
  (each).
Fresh foods are graded. If you want
top quality look for **Handelsklasse I,**
Hkl I, Kl I or **Kl A**. The price tag will
also give you the country of origin.

Blumenkohl
cauliflower

If you're buying pre-packed goods
look for **Paket** or **Pkt.** (packet),
Packung, Pckg. or **Pkg.** (carton or
pack). **Karton** (box), **Flasche** or **Fl.**
(bottle), **Glas** (jar), **Dose** (tin).

Riegel bars

Getting things done. . .

If you want something repaired watch
out for **repariert** or **Reparaturen**.

Uhren clocks, watches
Schmuck jewellery

For shoe repairs look for
Schuhreparaturen or signs mentioning
Absätze (heels).

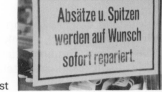

Spitzen tips
auf Wunsch on request

If you want to go to the hairdresser, find a **Friseur**, . . .**salon** or **Coiffeur** (the most high class type of hairdresser). Women look for **Damen**. . ., men for **Herren**. . .

. . . or cleaned

Launderettes are few and far between. So to get things washed or cleaned watch out for **Wäscherei** (laundry) and **Reinigung** (cleaners). Many offer a quick service (**Sofortdienst**, **Expressreinigung** or **Schnellreinigung**). Prices are displayed prominently in the window or on the outside of the shop.

Hose trousers
Rock skirt
Kleid dress
Jacke jacket
Mantel coat
Pulli jumper
gereinigt cleaned
gebügelt ironed

Shopping hours

Signs headed **Öffnungszeiten** or **Geschäftszeit(en)** give details of opening times. Normally shops close at 6.30 pm except on Saturdays, when they close around lunchtime. But on the first Saturday in every month (**langer Samstag** or **langer Sa**. = long Saturday) most shops stay open till about 6 pm. (For days of the week see p 10).

mit to   **Monat** month

Watch out for **geschlossen** (closed) and **durchgehend geöffnet** (open throughout the day). Some places have an early closing day, usually Wednesday afternoon (**Mittwoch nachmittag**).

The sign **Betriebsferien** or just **Ferien** tells you that the shop is closed for annual holidays.

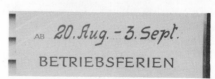

Buying from vending machines

When shops are closed you can often get what you need from a vending machine (**Automat**), for example, cigarettes (**Zigaretten**), matches (**Streichhölzer**), even flowers and snacks. Machines may be labelled **Kundendienst**, **Bedien Dich selbst** (serve yourself) etc. or give details of the goods for sale.

The slot where you put your money in may be marked **Einwurf** or you may be told to insert (**einwerfen**) money (**Geld**) or coins (**Münzen**).

Grosspackungen large packets
oder or
eine one

❓TEST YOURSELF

1 You want to buy (i) bread, (ii) meat and (iii) have a shirt washed. Which is the right place to go to?

a METZGEREI b Bäckerei c WÄSCHEREI

2 Three shops that sell food: what is the difference between them?

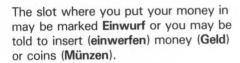

a FEINKOST b neuform HAUS Diät- und Reformwaren c Lebensmittel MILCH OBST · GEMÜSE

3 What do these signs advertise?

a Weinverkauf b Getränke Reiseandenken Süßwaren

4 You're dissatisfied with an article you bought. Is this the right counter to take it to?

ZENTRALKASSE · UMTAUSCH ·

80

5 At what times are these places open Mondays to Fridays?

a
Durchgehend geöffnet
8.15 – 18.00 Uhr
Samstag 9.00 – 12.30 Uhr

b

Geschäftszeiten
Montag - Freitag
6 30 - 12 30   14 30 - 18 30
Samstag 6 30 - 13 00
Mittwoch Nachmittag geschlossen

6 What would make you stop at

a this counter selling cassettes?

b this rack advertising blouses?

c this stall selling eggs?

d this butcher's?

7 If you were looking for something meaty, which of these signs would be helpful?

a

FLEISCHWAREN · SPEZIALITÄTEN

b
Mietwagen

c

FISCHE · WILD · GEFLÜGEL

Innocent abroad

AH! A GARDENING SHOP!

HOSE 2 90
ROCK 2 90
SACCO 3 70

81

11 EATING OUT AND DRINKING

KEY WORDS

Bier (beer)	see **Keller** and **Stube** below
Gast (guest, customer)	many words with . . .**gast**. . . indicate a restaurant: **Gasthaus**, **Gasthof** (inn, frequently with accommodation) **Gaststätte** (restaurant)
Keller (cellar)	tells you it's an eating or drinking place, often in the basement: **Bierkeller** (specialises in beer) **Ratskeller** (in basement of town hall – **Rathaus** – can be the best restaurant around) Note: **Rat** means council or advice, not 'rat'. **Weinkeller** (specialises in wines)
Speise (dish, food)	reminds you that you can get something to eat: **Speisekarte** (menu, often hung outside eating places) **Speisegaststätte**, **Speiserestaurant** (restaurant serving hot meals)
Stube (room)	a restaurant with an informal atmosphere; in Southern Germany you'll see the dialect version **Stübl** or **Stüberl**: **Bierstube** (serves beer and snacks) **Braustube**, **Braustüberl** (attached to a brewery – **brauen** = to brew) **Weinstube** (specialises in wines)
Tag (day)	**Mittagessen**, **Mittagstisch** (midday meal) **Ruhetag** (weekly closing day) **Tagesgericht** (dish of the day) Days of the week mostly end in . . .**tag**. (See p 10.)
Wein (wine)	see **Keller** and **Stube** above
Wurst (sausage)	may be the only hint that you can get a snack: **Bratwurst** (fried sausage) **Bockwurst** (large frankfurter i.e. boiled sausage) **Würstchen**, South German **Würstl** (small sausage)

If you want a meal

The main (hot) meal of the day is **Mittagessen** or **Mittagstisch**, served from noon till about 2.30 pm. In the evening most people have just bread, cheese and cold meats, but the larger restaurants are open for an evening meal (**Abendessen, Abendtisch**) from about 6.30 pm till around 9.30 pm.

For a family-type eating place with traditional decor, often serving regional dishes, look for signs with **Gasthaus**, **Gasthof**, **Gaststätte** (especially in a station or department store), **Ratskeller** or . . .**stube**. Some restaurant names start with **zum** or **zur** (here meaning 'at the sign of')

schwarzen Bären black bear
erbaut built

but sometimes **zum**, **zur** and **zu den** just point you in the right direction.

Many inns and restaurants are tied to a brewery (**Brauerei** or **Brauhaus**) and your first glimpse of an eating place may be a beer advert.

Hof court
Kegelbahn skittle alley

Just a snack

For a hot snack look for places advertising **warme Küche** (hot food), though many serve full meals as well.

Warme Küche von 12-18 Uhr

A **Café** (more like a tea room or coffee bar) also provides snacks. So do most restaurants outside meal times. For a quick snack look for **Imbiss** or **Schnellimbiss**. This may be an indoor snackbar, a kiosk or an outdoor stall (sometimes attached to a food shop).

There are also stalls advertising what they offer. Typical snacks are hot sausage eaten with bread (**Brot**) or a roll (**Brötchen**), chips (**Pommes frites** – yes, it's French!), soup (**Suppe**), rolls with different fillings (**belegte Brötchen**) etc. washed down with beer.

Limo = **Limonade** lemonade

Light refreshments in the afternoon

Many places advertise **Kaffee und Kuchen** (coffee and cake): it means that they serve cakes, pastries and drinks, including tea, in the afternoon.

The best place to go to is a **Konditorei** or **Café-Konditorei** where cakes and pastries (often with cream) are made on the premises. They also have ice-cream (**Eis**), hot and cold drinks but rarely alcohol.

Breakfast

If you want **Frühstück** (breakfast) the most likely place serving it is either a **Café** or a **Konditorei**.

bei Möhring at Möhring's

Just a drink

Wherever meals and snacks are served hot and cold drinks (including alcohol) are available. If you don't feel like eating, it's possible in many restaurants to order a drink only. For a place specialising in beer look for **Biergarten**, an open-air restaurant offering good plain food as well as other drinks, or **Bierkeller**, a plainly furnished hall geared to serving beer in huge quantities.

durchgehend all day

If you fancy draught beer watch out for **vom Fass** (from the barrel).

gut bürgerlicher good plain
Pils type of light beer

For a glass of local or new wine find a **Weinstube** (particularly in the wine-growing areas) or a **Weinkeller**. Both also sell food and other drinks.

Nest nest

A plain 'drinks only' place is **Ausschank** or **Schänke** (tavern).

Branntwein spirits

If you want to buy a drink from a stall or shop look for **Getränke** (drinks).

Süsswaren sweets

Buying ready-cooked food

You can buy this, often hot, from food shops and restaurants. The sign will say **Strassenverkauf** (street sale) or **zum Mitnehmen** (for taking away – not a direction sign or the name of a restaurant!).

For taking away
ready cooked
Portion of chips
with ketchup or mayonnaise
1 hot large frankfurter with roll
1 half portion of chicken
1 fillet of pork (in breadcrumbs)

Zum Mitnehmen
fertig zubereitet

Portion Pommesfrites	1.20
mit Ketchup od. Mayon.	1.50
1 heiße Bockwurst mit Brötchen	1.80
1 × ½ Hähnchen	4.80
1 Schweineschnitzel (paniert)	4.80

You can also get snacks from a vending machine (**Automat**). (See p 80.)

Refreshments on motorways (See chapter 2, p 34.)

Opening hours

There are no licensing hours, so **Cafés**, restaurants etc. can stay open well into the night. Many display their opening times. Look for **geöffnet ab** (open from), **Öffnungszeiten** (opening hours) and **durchgehend** (all day). Beware: most **Cafés** and restaurants close one day each week. The sign at the door will say **Ruhetag** or **Betriebsruhe** (closing day) (**Ruhe** = rest).

Heute
Ruhetag!

heute today

Jeden Montag
Betriebsruhe

jeden every

? TEST YOURSELF

1 What does the **Bratwurstglöckle** offer apart from rooms (**Fremdenzimmer**)?

2 Is your friend right when he says they only sell beer here?

3 You're ravenous. Any point in going up to this stall?

4 You're in the theatre. What sort of refreshments can you get in the foyer of the dress circle (**des 1.Ranges**)?

5 If you don't care for fried food which sausage would you buy?

a  b

6 Which of these advertises the name of a restaurant?

a

b  c

7 What meals can you get here?

a  b

8 If you like smoked trout (**geräucherte Forellen**) this sign will interest you. Why?

9 If you're keen on draught beer where would you be sure of getting it?

a

b

c

10 **Taverne** is the name of the disco — not a tavern, but you could get food there. (i) When? (ii) Are they open every day?

Innocent abroad

12 LOOKING FOR A LOO

TWO VITAL WORDS
frei (vacant)   **besetzt** (engaged)

How to recognise a loo

Other than **WC** or **Toilette(n)** you'll find
Abort

aussen outside   **neben** next to

You'll also come across the symbol OO for a loo and in Southern Germany, in particular, you may see this ♡ on a loo door in rural areas.

Women look for:
Damen, D, or **Frauen**

Men look for:
Herren, H, or **Männer**

Loos on motorways (See also p 34.)

Some lay-bys have WCs. Where there isn't one you're told how far away the next one is.

nächste nearest
Rastanlage service area
Pforzheim-Ost name of place
Sie finden you will find

You'll always find them in service areas.

Rasthaus motorway restaurant
Tankstellen petrol stations

What it costs

Women often have to pay, even in theatres, department stores etc. The usual charge (**Gebühr**) is 20 pfennigs.

Washing your hands (**Hände waschen**) —
and even combing your hair (**kämmen**) —
can cost extra.

When there is an attendant you may see
a door marked **Wartefrau** (even in the
gents) or its masculine equivalent **Wärter**
(in the gents only). Often you have to
cope with a coin-operated door lock and
put in 10-pfennig coins.

Careful! If you've not inserted the coins
before you go in you may not be able to
get out until you've put in the correct
money from inside.

Handtuch und Seife	0,20 DM
Kämmen	0,10 DM

Handtuch towel   **Seife** soap

> Erst 10 Pfg.-Münze
> einwerfen
> Dann Klinke ganz
> herunterdrücken

First insert 10-pfennig coin(s).
Then press handle right down.

❷TEST YOURSELF

1 Even if you're not sure what
öffentliches means what conclusion
would you draw from this sign?

2 If you can't find the sign **Männer**
which of these would be the right
one?

3 Would this door lead to the 'Ladies'?

4 What does this mean?

Kein öffentliches WC

Take heart — there are few signs as
diabolical as this one!

13 IF YOU FEEL ILL (See also chapter 14.)

⊕ KEY WORDS

Arzt (doctor)	**Ärztin** is the female equivalent **ärztlich** (medical)
	words ending in . . .**arzt/ärztin** usually describe specialist doctors: **Augenarzt** (eye specialist) **Facharzt** (specialist) **Frauenarzt** (gynaecologist) **Kinderarzt** (paediatrician) **Zahnarzt** (dentist) *but* **Tierarzt** is a vet!
Kasse (cash desk)	here short for **Krankenkasse** (see below)
krank (sick, ill)	**Krankenhaus** (hospital) **Krankheit** (illness, disease) **Krankenkasse** or **Kasse** (health insurance scheme) **Krankenwagen** (ambulance)
Not (need, emergency)	indicates something to be used in an emergency: **Notarzt** (doctor on call) **Notaufnahme** (Casualty Department) **Notdienst** (emergency service) **Notruf** (emergency phone)
Sprech. . . (**sprechen**, to speak)	has to do with when you can see a doctor: **Sprechstunde(n)** or **Sprechstd.** ⎫ **Sprechzeit(en)** or **Sprechz.** ⎭ (surgery hours)

If you need medicine or a simple remedy

Look for **Apotheke** (dispensing chemist's) or this (red) emblem.

These chemist's shops sell proprietary drugs and medicines (**Arzneimittel**), ointments, lotions, bandages etc. and sometimes dietary products (**Diät**) and body care preparations (**Körperpflege**). They dispense doctors' prescriptions (**Rezepte**) and will often give advice for minor ailments.

When the chemist's is closed (**geschlossen**) look for the sign **Notdienst der Apotheken**: it tells you which chemist's is open on which day *but* if you want toiletries, cosmetics etc. you normally need to find a **Drogerie**.

If you need a doctor

It's worth studying the doctor's sign beforehand. To be sure he or she is a Doctor of Medicine look for **Dr.med**. A GP is often called **prakt.Arzt/Ärztin** or **Arzt/Ärztin für Allgemeinmedizin** (general medicine).

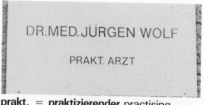

prakt. = **praktizierender** practising

The sign may also tell you if the doctor is a specialist (**Facharzt/ärztin**) and what he or she specialises in.

Augenkrankheiten eye diseases

If you have toothache

Look for **Zahnarzt** or **Zahnärztin**. They are plain **Dr.** or known merely by their name. As a rule they will see you only by appointment (**nach Vereinbarung**).

Aufzug lift   **Etage** floor

To find out about surgery hours

Look on the doctor's sign for **Sprechstunde(n)**, **Sprechstd.** or **Sprechzeit(en)**, **Sprechz.**, followed by the day (see p 10) and time.

alle all

Cutting the cost

See if it says **alle Kassen** on the sign: it means that you can get free treatment (but only with the appropriate form from your local Department of Health and Social Security). Beware: many doctors and dentists take only private patients (**nur privat**), and fees are high.

If you have to go to a hospital

Follow the sign **Krankenhaus** or **Klinik**.

To call an ambulance (Krankenwagen) see p 95.

If you need first aid see p 94.

❓ TEST YOURSELF

1 If you have toothache who is the right specialist? Could you get free
  treatment?

a

Gerhard Bräuer
Zahnarzt
Sprechstunden nach Vereinbarung
Alle Kassen

b
Dr. med. vet. Beust
Tierarzt

c
Sanitätsrat Dr. W. Brust
Arzt für Allgemeinmedizin

2 You prefer to consult a woman doctor. Which key word helps you
  choose the right one?

a

Dr. med.
Katja Obenaus
prakt. Ärztin
alle Kassen

b
DR. MED. F. WITTE
FRAUENARZT

3 You have a bad cold. Which sign should you follow to get a quick
  remedy?

a

ZUR APOTHEKE
BEIM RATHAUS

b
Stadtklinik

4 When does this doctor see patients?

SPRECHSTUNDE TÄGLICH 15-17⁰⁰
UND NACH VEREINBARUNG
SAMSTAG KEINE SPRECHSTUNDE

5 Is this a man or a woman? A doctor
  or a dentist?

DR. G. WALTER - KNOBLOCH
FACHZAHNÄRZTIN FÜR KIEFER-
ORTHOPÄDIE

Take a closer look at this one. Anything
unusual about it? Would it be outside a
doctor's house? (You may need to
consult your dictionary!)

Zum
DOKTOR
Facharzt für durstige Kehlen
alle Kassen
Sprechstunden von 16⁰⁰ - 1⁰⁰

14 DANGERS AND EMERGENCIES

(See also chapter 13.)

🔑 KEY WORDS

Feuer
(fire)

Feuergefahr (see **Gefahr** below)
Feuermelder (fire alarm)
Feuerwehr (fire brigade)

Gefahr
(danger)

words with . . .**gefahr, gefähr**. . . warn you of risks
and dangers:
Brandgefahr, Feuer(s)gefahr (fire risk)
Diebstahlgefahr (beware of thieves)
gefährdet (endangered)
Gefahrenzone (danger zone)
gefährlich (dangerous)
Lebensgefahr (danger to life)
bei Gefahr (in case of danger

Not
(need, emergency)

indicates something to be used in an emergency:
Notarzt (doctor on call)
Notausfahrt (emergency exit for vehicles)
Notausgang (emergency exit if you're on foot)
Notdienst (emergency service)
Notruf (emergency phone, emergency call)
bei Not, im Notfall (in case of emergency)

Unfall
(accident)

Unfallarzt (doctor treating accident cases)
Unfallbrennpunkt (accident black spot)
Unfallhilfsstelle (first aid post)

Steering clear of danger

There are many signs warning you of
serious risk of accident or injury. (Many
others are put up to absolve the owner/s
of legal liability if you do have an
accident.) These signs usually include
. . .**gefahr** and often **Vorsicht** or
Achtung.

Hochspannung high voltage

Tollwut rabies   **Bezirk** area

You'll also come across warnings about dangers caused by wintry weather.

bei Sturm und Schnee in stormy and snowy weather
Umgebung des Domes surroundings of the cathedral

but **auf eigene Gefahr** merely tells you that you're doing something at your own risk that may not be at all dangerous.

Waldparkplatz car park in woodland

An exclamation mark can also be a danger warning.
So can **Warnung** (warning) and **Warndienst** (warning service).

When things go wrong

You may need to find the emergency exit. Look for **Notausgang** if you're on foot, for **Notausfahrt** if you're driving.

freihalten keep clear

You may need police help. If there is no phone or emergency call box nearby (see next page) try to find the nearest police station signposted **Polizei** or **Polizeiwache**, or a police patrol car.

If you need first aid

First aid posts are run by the **Malteser** (similar to St John Ambulance) and the Red Cross (**Deutsches Rotes Kreuz** known as **DRK**, or in Bavaria as **BRK**, i.e. **Bayerisches Rotes Kreuz**).

Sometimes a first aid post is signposted **Sanitätsstation** or **Rettungshilfsstelle** (**retten** = to rescue, **Hilfe** = help).

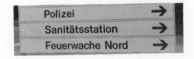

Watch out for signs saying **Unfallarzt, Notarzt, Notdienst** and those directing you to a hospital (**Krankenhaus** or **Klinik**).

. . . or an ambulance

You call the emergency services (see below) or the **DRK** or **BRK**. Remember you have to pay for an ambulance (**Krankenwagen**) or for one with special life-saving equipment (**Rettungswagen**).

To call the emergency services

From a telephone

You can summon help from any telephone by dialling 110, the number for **Notruf** (emergency): this connects you with the police, ambulance service, flying squad etc. In case of fire, 112 puts you through to the fire brigade (**Feuerwehr**).

In ordinary public phone boxes (they are yellow) you need two **10-Pfennig** coins even for an emergency call.

From a free emergency phone

Free emergency calls can be made from public phone boxes with two red bands marked **Münzfreier Notruf** (see p 55). These call boxes have extra equipment next to the normal telephone, with complicated instructions unlikely to be read in an emergency. The essential thing is to lift the receiver and move the lever to the right (**Hebel nach rechts bewegen**) for the police, ambulance etc.,

– to the left (**nach links**) for the fire brigade (**Feuerwehr**).

On the motorway

Look for the orange-coloured emergency phones which put you in touch with the local motorway control centre (**Autobahnmeisterei**). (See chapter 2, p 34.)

❷ TEST YOURSELF

1 Under what circumstances would you follow this sign?

2 What do you have to do in an
emergency?

3 This sign at a camp site draws your
attention to the use of electricity.
What does it say about it?

4 You're being warned. Why?

a  b  c

5 Your friend has cut his finger badly.
Any point following any of these
signs?

6 Which of these emergency numbers
would you call (i) in case of fire (ii) if
there's a burglary (iii) in case of an
accident?

7 Which emergency service can you
call from this machine? What does it
cost? What should you do with the
lever?

Answers to 'Test yourself' questions

Finding your way through the forest of signs

1 and 2 (Words in brackets give you the clue to the signs.)

  (i) **b** 'please don't smoke' (**bitte nicht**); (ii) **f** 'please always close this door' (**bitte**); (iii) **c** 'beware barrier' (**Achtung!**); (iv) **e** 'trade fair' (one-word sign); (v) **a** 'no entry' (**kein**); (vi) **d** 'no parking' (**verboten**).

3 and 4 (Words in brackets give you the clue.)

  (i) **b** 'for hotel guests only' (**nur**); (ii) **e** 'no dogs (**Hunden**) allowed'; (iii) **c** 'open Sunday — Friday 7.30 am — 1 am; Saturday 7.30 am — 3 am' (**geöffnet**); (iv) **d** 'children — playground — music' (**Kinder**); (v) **a** 'day tickets — adults 2.50 marks — children up to 4 years free of charge' (**Tageskarten**); (vi) **f** 'tickets — air tickets — ferry boats' (**Fahrkarten**).

5 **a** prohibition: **verboten** ('no smoking'); **b** (emphatic) instruction: **zu führen** ('dogs must be kept on a lead'); **c** instruction: **Knopf. . .drücken** ('when coins have dropped, push button hard'); **d** prohibition: **nicht erlaubt** ('cycling not allowed' — **dies ist** = this is); **e** prohibition: **nicht gestattet** ('radio and other musical instruments not permitted'); **f** prohibition: **untersagt** ('the use of mopeds, motorised cycles and cycles in the shopping centre is forbidden').

Chapter

---

1 1 **b** 'to the office'.   2 you shouldn't go through (**Durchgang für Fussgänger** = way through for pedestrians).   3 'please don't ring — push door'.   4 **a** 'entrance round the corner'; **b** you shouldn't cross the road here (**kein Übergang** = no crossing), but cross where the arrow points to.   5 **a** none — unless you have a dog with you; **b** 'visitors must report to reception' (**müssen sich anmelden** = must report themselves). 6 **a** right (**Zugang rechts** = access on the right); **b** left (**linken Durchgang** = way through on the left).   7 by taking the footpath (**Fussgängerweg**).   8 **a** you use it at your own risk; **b** out of (**ausser**) action (**Betrieb**) (**Wir bitten um Verständnis** = we apologise for the inconvenience).   9 **a** unauthorised persons are not allowed to go on it; **b** you go over it at your own risk.   Innocent: **Ausgang** (exit) marks the spot on the landing stage where passengers disembark.

2a 1 **a** bridge across the Rhine; **b** airport; **c** straight on to Radolfzell, to the right to Konstanz and the car ferry (**Auto-Fähre**).   2 tractors (**ausgen.** = **ausgenommen**).   3 to switch off the engine.   4 if you're a visitor, you may not drive through (**keine Durchfahrt**); parking only in the car park.   5 'get in lane' (**einordnen**). 6 **a** pedestrian precinct (**Fussgängerstrasse**); **b** oncoming traffic (**Begegnungsverkehr**) for (**auf**) 1200 metres; **c** traffic on the left (**Linksverkehr**) (**nur Schritt fahren** = dead slow).   7 **Zufahrt . . .frei**.   8 'please keep your distance' (**ich bremse auch für Tiere** = I even brake for animals).   9 buses, trams, taxis, residents' vehicles.   10 to the car park.

---

b 1 **a** cars, motorcycles, bicycles; **b** cars; post office customers (**Postkunden**); **c** hire cars.   2 left, where it says **Kurzparker**.   3 two-wheelers.   4 under-cover car park; open until 1 am; entrance for vehicles up to 2 metres high.   5 80 pfennigs an hour; stop (**anhalten**).   6 (i) **a** and **b** (ii) **a** yes (**gebührenpflichtig**); **b** no; **c** 1 mark an hour, but it's full (**besetzt**).   7 (i) parking disc; (ii) 12 noon i.e. 2 hours (**2 Stunden**).   8 **b** (**a** warns you of a dog).   9 it might get towed away (**abgeschleppt**) at your expense (**kostenpflichtig**).

c 1 **b** and **c** (**a** shows an expressway (**Autostrasse**) to the town centre).
2 **a** indicates a relief road from a motorway eventually leading back to it; **b** motorway intersection 2 kilometres ahead, nearest town Bad Dürrheim; **c** two motorways cross 750 metres ahead, nearest town Böblingen. 3 (i) yes; (ii) **a Rastplatz** = lay-by (**Am Kahlenberg** – name of locality); **b Raststätte** points to a motorway restaurant.

d 1 self-service pump. 2 oil change. 3 (i) **c**; (ii) **d**; (iii) **a**; (**b** is a car wash). 4 at the cash desk. 5 (i) yes (**Batteriedienst** = battery service); (ii) no; (iii) yes (**Reifendienst** = tyre service). Innocent: **Ausfahrt** = motorway exit.

3 1 **a** underground station; **b** bus stop (**Stadtverkehr** = municipal service). 2 **a** buses; **b** buses (**Omnibusse**) and the suburban line (symbol **S**). 3 buses go in the direction of Konstanz. 4 single journey tickets; strip of tickets. 5 you can only board with a valid (**gültigem**) ticket; tickets are not sold in the vehicle. Innocent: sign inside bus means 'change returned here'.

4 1 'no train information given here – opposite (**gegenüber**) platform 21 only'. 2 **Autoreisezug**. 3 **b** 'to the left luggage lockers'; (**a** sends you to the exit and platforms 1, 4, 5; **c** to the trains). 4 to the ticket office (**Fahrkarten**) and the trains (**zu den Zügen**) going in the direction of Kaiserslautern. 5 no – it should say **Warteraum** or **Wartesaal**. 6 (i) **a** and **b** (**Ausland** and **Auslandsverkehr** are the clues); (ii) **b** it says **Platzkarten**. 7 a place selling newspapers and magazines, cigarettes and tobacco, and sweets; a station restaurant. 8 buy a ticket (**Fahrkartenausgabe**); leave/collect luggage (**Gepäck**). Innocent: **Kinderwagen** = prams (**Traglasten** = bulky objects).

5 1 in the tourist office (**Verkehrsbüro**). 2 provides bed and breakfast only. 3 **a** 'rooms vacant'; **b** also advertises rooms but they are taken (**besetzt**). 4 campers only. 5 prohibition (**untersagt** is the clue): you're not allowed to wash up (**abwaschen**) crockery. 6 no noise permitted at these times (**Ruhe** = rest period, but it can also mean 'quiet').

6 1 Monday 10 am. 2 (i) **Telegramme** and (ii) **Sondermarken** (for (iii) you need to look for **Paketannahme**). 3 (i) counter 11 (**Ferngespräche**); (ii) counter 2 (**Postwertzeichen kl.Mengen**); (iii) counter 2 (**postlagernde Sendungen**); (iv) counter 2 (**Einschreibsendungen**). You can ignore counter 6. 4 when it doesn't work. 5 a letter box with frequent collections (the dot tells you); **b** phone box for making free calls to the emergency services. Innocent: it's the name of an inn (**Gasthof**) – **Post** = post house.

7 1 **b**; (**a** is a casino). 2 yes, until 6 pm (**Donnerstag verlängert bis** = Thursday extended until). 3 (i) no (**Wechsel** = bill of exchange); (ii) yes, it says **Geldwechsel** (exchange bureau). 4 small change. 5 insert a 1-mark coin. Innocent: **Fundbüro** = lost property office.

8 1 **Rathaus** (town hall), **Museum**. 2 **a** mountain railway (**Merkur**, name of mountain); **b** the new (**neu**) and old (**alt**) castle. 3 **Olympia-Turm** (tower). 4 round trips by motor boat. 5 **a** at the ticket counter; **b** on board (**auf den Schiffen**). 6 to visit Favorite Palace (**besucht** or **besuchen Sie** = visit); **das unberührte Denkmal** = the unspoilt monument, **18. Jahrh.** = 18th century. 7 total DM 4.60 (i.e. two adults DM 3.-; one 12-year old 0.80; one student 0.80). 8 every day except Mondays (**Montag geschlossen**); photos and films, puppet theatres, musical instruments, German brewery (**Brauerei**) museum. Innocent: a misreading of **beim** = near the; 'at the' would be **im**.

9 1 **a** car park for visitors to the national park called **Pfälzerwald**; **b** marked footpath along the German wine route; **c** path from Baden-Baden to Offenburg through the wine-growing Ortenau area.   2 **b Badezentrum** (**a** says you're not allowed to swim – baden. . . **nicht gestattet**; **c** means spa treatment in hot spring water).   3 DM 4.- i.e. your daughter pays full rate (**bis 14 J.** = up to age 14).   4 **b** (**a** 'men – to the pool').   5 **a** 'please don't dive into the water'; **b** 'for divers only'.   6 **a** dismount (**absteigen**); **b** use the cycle stands (**Fahrradständer**). (The rest says you're not allowed to lean bicycles against the wall.)   7 **a** to skateboard and cycle in the passage; **b** play ball games (**Ballspielen**). (The rest tells you that it's a bathing beach, not a football ground, and that music is not welcome.)   Innocent: **grillen** means 'grilling or barbecueing food'.

10 1 (i) **b**; (ii) **a**; (iii) **c**.   2 **a** sells select food; **b** diet and health foods; **c** groceries, milk, fruit and vegetables.   3 **a** wine; **b** drinks, souvenirs, sweets.   4 yes, it says **Umtausch** (exchange).   5 **a** all day (**durchgehend**); **b** mornings and afternoons, but closed Wednesday afternoon.   6 **a Preisknüller** (fabulous offer); **b Sonderpreis** (special price); **c Angebot der Woche** (this week's offer); **d Einkaufstip** (best buy). 7 **a** and **c** (**b** is an advert for hire cars – **mieten** = to hire, **Wagen** = car, *not* a misprint for **Waren**!).   Innocent: **Hose** is not a hose, but trousers; **Rock** doesn't mean 'rock' but 'skirt'; **Sacco** isn't a sack, but a man's jacket. It's a dry-cleaners.

11 1 a restaurant serving beer, wine and hot food.   2 no – it's a restaurant advertising good plain food (**gut bürgerliche Gaststätte**).   3 yes – there's a stall selling snacks and sweets.   4 drinks and sweets.   5 **a** (**b** are fried sausages).   6 **b** and **c** (**a** points the way to the canteen).   7 **a** breakfast; **b** midday and evening meal (**Qualitätsweine** = select wines, **Spez.** = **Spezialität** speciality, **Bodenseefische** = fish from Lake Constance).   8 you can buy them to take away (**zum Mitnehmen**); **frisch** = freshly.   9 **b** it advertises **König-Pilsener** (type of beer) **vom Fass**.   10 (i) from 8.30 pm – 2 am; (ii) no – closed on Monday.   Innocent: Wolf is the name of the snackbar.

12 1 you can't go there (**kein** = no, gives you the clue – **öffentliches** = public). 2 **H** for **Herren** (gents).   3 no – to the lavatory attendant.   4 public loo. Last sign: 'WC facilities can be reached via the cemetery through the waiting room near the tomb of Ulrika'.

13 1 **a Zahnarzt** = dentist (**b** is a vet; **c** a GP. **Sanitätsrat** is an honorary title); you could get free treatment: it says **alle Kassen**.   2 **a Ärztin** = woman doctor (**b Frauenarzt** = gynaecologist).   3 **a** 'to the chemist's near the town hall' (**b** points to the municipal hospital).   4 every day between 3 – 5 pm and by appointment, no surgery on Saturdays.   5 woman (. . .**ärztin**); dental specialist (**Fachzahnärztin**). Last sign: 'To the doctor – specialist for thirsty throats – all health insurance schemes – surgery hours from 6 pm – 1 am'. Note: **Kasse** is a pun – it also means 'cash'. The sign is outside a night club!

14 1 when you need to find a fire alarm (**Feuermelder**).   2 you have to open here in case of danger (**bei Gefahr**).   3 you use it at your own risk (**auf eigene Gefahr**). 4 **a** there could be a storm (**Sturmwarndienst** = storm warning service); **b** there's an exit for vehicles; **c** there's a risk of rabies in the area.   5 yes – **DRK Klinik** (Red Cross hospital).   6 (i) 112 (you can also contact the fire brigade if you dial 110); (ii) 110; (iii) 110 for an ambulance, also 22222 for a Red Cross ambulance 22105 for a doctor; the small print tells you there's a first aid kit at the entrance. 7 fire brigade (**Feuerwehr**); free of charge(**kein Geld einwerfen**); you turn the lever to the left (**links**).

Word list

The meanings listed here apply to words used on signs included in this book; other meanings are not listed. Shorter forms are given in brackets. The numbers in brackets refer you to the page on which the word is explained more fully. Note that in German all nouns start with a capital letter.

a. = **am** or **an**
ab from, departing from
Abendtisch evening meal
Abfahrt departure
Abgastest exhaust testing
abgeschleppt towed away
abgestellt parked
abnehmen to lift
Abstand distance
absteigen to dismount
abstellen to switch off; to leave, park
abwaschen to wash up
Achtung beware
alle all
Allgemeinmedizin general medicine
alt old
am (**a.**) on the, at the
an (**a.**) on, at, arriving at
Angebot offer
angezeigt reported
anhalten to stop
Ankunft arrival
Anlage gardens; facility
anlehnen to lean against something
Anlieger(verkehr) residents' (vehicles)
anmelden to report
Anmeldung reception
Annahme place for handing in goods, money etc.
Apotheke dispensing chemist's (90)
Art kind
Arzt doctor (90)
Ärztin woman doctor
auch even, also
auf on, on to, for
Aufbewahrung storage
Aufforderung request
Ausblick view

Ausfahrt exit, way out (for vehicles)
Ausflug/Ausflüge excursion/s
Ausgabe place for collecting (goods, mail etc.); change given
Ausgang exit, way out (for pedestrians)
ausgegeben issued
ausgenommen (**ausgen.**) except
Auskunft information
Ausland abroad
Auslandsverkehr foreign travel
ausser Betrieb out of order
Aussicht view
Aussichtspunkt vantage point
Ausstieg exit (in bus, tram etc.)
Autobahn motorway
Autobahndreieck, Autobahnkreuz motorway intersection (32)
Autofähre car ferry
Autoreisezug motorail
autorisiert authorised
Autostrasse expressway
Autovermietung car hire
Autowäsche car wash

Bäckerei bakery
Bad. = **Badisch(er)** from Baden (name of Federal state)
Bad bathroom; pool; bath; spa (69)
Badegelände, Badeplatz, Badestelle bathing area
baden to bathe; bathing
Badestrand bathing beach

Badezentrum swimming centre
Bahnhof (**Bf.**, **Bhf.**) station
Bahnhof(s)gaststätte station restaurant
bedienen to serve
Bedienung service
Befahren riding
Begegnungsverkehr oncoming traffic
bei at; in case of
beim near the; when
belegt filled; full
Beleuchtungstest testing of lights
benutzen, benützen to use
Benutzung, Benützung use
Benzin petrol; two star petrol
Beratung advice
bereit ready
Bergbahn mountain railway
besetzt full, taken; engaged
Besichtigung visit
besuchen to visit
Besucher visitor/s
betreten to step on to (8)
Betrieb works, business
bewegen to move
bezahlen to pay
Bezirk area
Bhf. = **Bahnhof** station
Bier beer
bis until, up to
bitte please
Blick view
Bockwurst boiled sausage, frankfurter
Bodensee Lake Constance
Bootfahren boating
Bratwurst fried sausage
Brauerei brewery
bremsen to brake

Briefe letters
Briefeinwurf slot for posting letters
Brötchen bread roll/s
Brücke bridge
Burg castle, palace (61)
Büro office
Busfahrt bus trip
Busse buses

ca. = **circa** approximately
Campingbesucher visitor/s to a camp site
Campinggäste campers

Damen (D) 'ladies'
das the
DDR = **Deutsche Demokratische Republik** East Germany
dem to the, of the
den the, to the
Denkmal monument
der the, of the
des of the
Di. = **Dienstag** Tuesday
Diätwaren dietary products
die the
Diebstahl theft
Dienst service
Dienstag (Die., Di.) Tuesday
diese this
DM = **Deutsche Mark**
Donnerstag (Do.) Thursday
DRK = **Deutsches Rotes Kreuz** German Red Cross
Drogerie chemist's selling toiletries etc.
drücken to press, push
durch through, by
Durchfahrt way through (for vehicles)
Durchgang way through (for pedestrians)
durchgehend all day
dürfen may
D-Zug fast train

E = **Entwerter** or **Eilzug**
Ecke corner
  um die Ecke round the corner
Eier eggs
Eilzug semi-fast train

ein a, an
Einfahrt entry, way in (for vehicles)
Eingang entry, way in (for pedestrians)
Einkaufstip best buy
Einkaufszentrum (EKZ) shopping centre
einordnen to get in lane
Einschreibsendungen registered mail
Einstieg entrance (buses)
Eintritt entrance, admission (13)
Eintrittspreise admission charges
einwerfen to insert
Einwurf slot for inserting coins
Einzelfahrkarten tickets for a single journey
Einzelkabine single cabin, cubicle
EKZ = **Einkaufszentrum** shopping centre
entfernt towed away
entnehmen to remove
entwerten to cancel (41)
Entwerter (E) ticket cancelling machine
erlaubt allowed
Erwachsene adults
Expressgut express parcel service

Facharzt specialist (doctor)
Fachzahnärztin woman dental specialist
Fahrausweis ticket
Fahrbahn roadway, carriageway
Fähre ferry
fahren to travel; to drive
Fahrkarte ticket for train, bus etc.
Fahrkartenausgabe, Fahrkartenschalter ticket office
Fahrpreis fare
Fahrräder bicycles
Fahrradständer cycle stand/s
Fahrschein ticket for train, bus etc.

Fahrt journey, trip
Fahrtreppe escalator
Fahrzeug vehicle
Fass barrel
feiertags on public holidays
Feinkost select foods
Ferien holidays
Ferngespräche long-distance phone calls
Fernsprecher telephone
fest firmly
Feuer fire, naked lights
Feuermelder fire alarm
Feuerwache, Feuerwehr fire brigade
Fleischwaren meat products
Flughafen airport
Flugscheine airline tickets
Fr. = **Freitag** Friday
Frauen women
Frauenarzt gynaecologist
frei free, available; exempt, allowed; clear
freihalten to keep clear
Freitag (Frei., Fr.) Friday
Fremdenzimmer guest room/s, room/s to let
frisch fresh(ly)
Friseur hairdresser
Frühstück breakfast
führen to lead
Fundbüro lost property office
für (f.) for
Fussballplatz football ground
Fussgänger pedestrian/s
Fussgängerstrasse pedestrian precinct
Fussgängerweg footpath
Fussweg footpath

garni: Hotel garni bed and breakfast hotel
Gärten gardens
Gasthaus inn
Gasthof inn
Gaststätte restaurant
Gästezimmer guest room/s
Gebühr charge
gebührenfrei free of charge
gebührenpflichtig charge payable

Gefahr danger
auf eigene Gefahr at
your risk
gefährdet endangered
gefallen dropped
Geflügel poultry
gegenüber opposite
Gehweg pavement
Geld money, coins
Geldwechsel exchange
bureau
Gemüse vegetables
geöffnet open
Gepäck luggage
Geschäftszeit(en) business
hours
Geschirr crockery
geschlossen closed
gesperrt closed to traffic
Gespräche phone calls
gestattet permitted
Getränke drinks
Gleis platform
gr. = Gramm gram
gross great, large
gültig valid
gut good; well
gut bürgerlich good plain

h = Uhr o'clock
H = Haltestelle stop
haben to have
Halle hall
halt stop
halten to keep, hold
Hauptbahnhof (Hbf.) main
station
Hauptstrasse high street
Haus/Häuser house/s;
shop/s
Hebel lever
Herren (H) men, gents
heute today
hier here
Hof yard, court; = Gasthof
inn
Hörer receiver
Hose trousers
Hotelgäste hotel guests
Hund dog

ich I
Ihr your
im in the, on the

Imbiss snack, snack bar
immer always
Innenstadt town centre
ist is

Jahre (J.) years old
Jahrh. = Jahrhundert
century
je each
jede each, every
Jugendherberge youth
hostel

Kasse cash desk, cashier's;
ticket office; health
insurance scheme (90)
Kassenschluss time of last
admission
kein no
Kieferorthopädie
orthodontics
Kinder children
Kinderspielplatz children's
playground
kl. = klein small
Kleingeld small change
Klinik hospital
Knopf button
Konditorei cake shop
kostenpflichtig at owner's
expense
Kräder = Kraftfahrräder
motorcycles
Krankenhaus hospital
Krankenwagen ambulance
Kreuz cross(roads)
Küche food, cooking
Kunden customers
Kurpark gardens in a spa
Kurve bend
Kurzparker drivers using
short-stay car park

Laden shop
lagern to camp; camping
läuten to ring
Lebensmittel food,
groceries
leer blank
Leerung postal collection
Leine lead
links left, on the left
Lkw = Lastkraftwagen
lorry (27)

Luft air
Männer men
Markt market
Mehrfahrtenkarten strips of
tickets
Mengen amounts
Messe trade fair; Mass
Metzgerei butcher's
Mietwagen hire car/s
Milch milk
mit (m.) with, by
mitbringen to take along
mitnehmen to take away
Mittagessen midday meal
Mittagsruhe afternoon quiet
period (50)
Mittagstisch midday meal
Mittwoch (Mi.) Wednesday
Mofas = Motorfahrräder
motorised cycles
Montag (Mo.) Monday
Motor engine
Motorboot motor boat
Motorzünddiagnose ignition
check
Münze coin
Münzeinwurf slot for
inserting coins
münzfrei no coins needed
Münzrückgabe return of
coins
Münzwechsler coin-
changing machine
müssen to have to

nach to; by; after
Nachmittag afternoon
nächste next, nearest
Nachtruhe nighttime quiet
period
Naturpark national park,
beauty spot
Naturschutzgebiet nature
reserve
neu new
nicht no, not, non-
Notruf emergency phone
(34, 95); emergency (95)
Nr. = Nummer number
nur only

Obergeschoss upper floor
Obst fruit
oder (od.) or

öffentlich public
öffnen to open
Öffnungszeiten opening times
Ölstand oil level
Ölwechsel oil change
Omnibusse buses
Opernhaus opera house
Ost east

Paket parcel
parken to park; parking
Parkgarage multi-storey car park
Parkgebühr parking fee
Parkplatz car park; parking space
Parkschein ticket for parking
Pf., Pfg. = Pfennig
Pils light beer
Pkw = Personen-kraftwagen car (27)
Platz square; seat; area, place
Platzkarten seat reservations
Polizei police
polizeilich by order of the police
Post post office; post house
postlagernd 'poste restante'
Postwertzeichen postage stamp/s
prakt. = praktizierend practising
Preise prices, charges
Preisknüller fabulous offer
pro per
Puppentheater puppet theatre

radfahren to cycle; cycling
Radfahrer cyclist/s
Rang circle (in theatre)
Rastanlage service area
Rasthaus, Rasthof motorway inn
Rastplatz lay-by
Raststätte motorway inn
Rathaus town hall
rauchen to smoke, smoking
rechts right, on the right
Reformwaren health foods

Reifendienst tyre service
Reise trip, journey
Reiseandenken souvenir/s
Reisebüro travel agency
Reisegepäck heavy luggage
Reisezugauskunft train travel information
Rhein Rhine
Richtung direction
Rock skirt
Rolltreppe escalator
Rückfahrt return journey
Rückgabe return (of coins)
Ruhetag weekly closing day
Rundfahrt round trip

S = S-Bahn suburban line
Sa. = Samstag Saturday
Sacco jacket
Sammlung collection
Samstag (Samst., Sa.) Saturday
SB = selbst (your)self
Schalterstunden, Schalterzeiten banking hours
Scheck cheque/s
Schiff ship, boat, steamer
Schiffslände landing stage
schliessen to close
Schliessfächer luggage lockers
Schloss/Schlösser castle/s, palace/s (61)
Schlüssel key
schnell quick(ly)
Schranke barrier
Schritt walking pace
Schwimmhalle indoor swimming pool
selbst (your)self
Sendungen mail
sich oneself, themselves
Sie you
sind are
so this way
So. = Sonntag Sunday
sofort immediately
Sommer summer
Sondermarken commemorative stamps
Sonderpreis special price

Sonntag (So.) Sunday
sonstige other
Speise food, dish
Sperrzone area closed to traffic
Spielbank casino
spielen to play
Spielplatz playground
Sprechstunden surgery hours
springen to dive
Springer diver/s
Stadt town
städtisch (städt.) municipal
Stadtmitte town centre
Stadtschänke name of a tavern
Std. = Stunde hour
stimmt is correct
Strasse (Str.) street, road; scenic route
Strassenbahn tram
Stromentnahme use of electricity
Stück (St.) piece; each
Stunde (Std.) hour
Sturm storm
Süsswaren sweets; sweetshop

Tabak tobacco
Tafel bar (of chocolate); board
Tageskarten day tickets
täglich (tägl., tgl.) daily
Tank (petrol) pump
Tankbeleg bill for petrol
Thermalbäder hot baths in spa
Tiefgarage underground car park
Tierarzt vet
Tiere animals
Tiergarten zoo
Tollwut rabies
Tür door
Turm tower

u. = und and
U = Umleitung diversion;
= Untergrundbahn underground railway
Übergang crossing, way across (for pedestrians)

Uhr o'clock
um round
Umtausch exchange of
 goods
Unbefugte unauthorised
 persons
unberechtigt illegally
unberührt unspoilt
und (u.) and
unerwünscht not welcome
Unfallarzt doctor treating
 accident cases
untersagt prohibited

v. = von from, of
Verbandkasten first aid kit
Verbot prohibition
verboten forbidden
Vereinbarung appointment
Verkauf sale
Verkehr traffic; travel
Verkehrsamt, Verkehrsbüro
 tourist office
verlängert extended
Versagen failure
Verständnis understanding
vom from the
von (v.) from, of
vor before, in front of
Vorsicht beware

Wagen car
wählen to select; to dial
Wald wood(land)
Wanderweg marked
 footpath

Waren goods
warm hot
Warndienst warning service
Warnung (vor) beware (of)
Wartefrau (woman)
 lavatory attendant
Warteraum, Wartesaal
 waiting room
Wartung service
Wäscherei laundry
Wasser water
Wechsel change,
 exchange; bill of
 exchange (56)
Wechselgeld (small) change
Wechselstube exchange
 bureau
Weg way, path
Wegweiser sign board
Wein wine
Weinkeller restaurant
 specialising in wine
Weinlesefest wine
 harvesting festival
Weinpfad path through
 wine-growing area
Weinstube restaurant
 specialising in wine
wenn when
werden will be; be
werktags on weekdays
Wertsendungen valuables
 by registered mail
widerrechtlich illegally
Wild game

willkommen welcome
Winzerfest wine growers'
 festival
wir we
wird will be
Woche week
Wohnung flat
Wohnwagen caravan

Zahnarzt dentist
Zeit time
Zeitschriften newspapers
 and periodicals
Zentralkasse main cash
 desk
Zimmer room/s
Zimmernachweis
 accommodation bureau
zu to
zu den, zum, zur to the;
 at the sign of (83)
Zufahrt access (for
 vehicles)
Zug/Züge train/s
Zugang access (for
 pedestrians)
Zugauskunft train
 information
Zugmaschinen tractors
zurück return, back
Zutritt access (13)
Zweiräder two-wheelers
Zweiradfahrer cyclist/s,
 motor cyclists